Public Pensions,
Capital Formation,
and Economic Growth

Westview Replica Editions

The concept of Westview Replica Editions is a response to the continuing crisis in academic and informational publishing. Library budgets for books have been severely curtailed. Ever larger portions of general library budgets are being diverted from the purchase of books and used for data banks, computers, micromedia, and other methods of information retrieval. Interlibrary loan structures further reduce the edition sizes required to satisfy the needs of the scholarly community. Economic pressures (particularly inflation and high interest rates) on the university presses and the few private scholarly publishing companies have severely limited the capacity of the industry to properly serve the academic and research communities. As a result, many manuscripts dealing with important subjects, often representing the highest level of scholarship, are no longer economically viable publishing projects--or, if accepted for publication, are typically subject to lead times ranging from one to three years.

Westview Replica Editions are our practical solution to the problem. We accept a manuscript in camera-ready form, typed according to our specifications, and move it immediately into the production process. As always, the selection criteria include the importance of the subject, the work's contribution to scholarship, and its insight, originality of thought, and excellence of exposition. The responsibility for editing and proofreading lies with the author or sponsoring institution. We prepare chapter headings and display pages, file for copyright, and obtain Library of Congress Cataloging in Publication Data. A detailed manual contains simple instructions for preparing the final typescript, and our editorial staff is always available to answer questions.

The end result is a book printed on acid-free paper and bound in sturdy library-quality soft covers. We manufacture these books ourselves using equipment that does not require a lengthy make-ready process and that allows us to publish first editions of 300 to 600 copies and to reprint even smaller quantities as needed. Thus, we can produce Replica Editions quickly and can keep even very specialized books in print as long as there is a demand for them.

About the Book and Author

Public Pensions, Capital Formation, and Economic Growth
Miltiadis Nektarios

Dr. Nektarios examines the principles and criteria underlying public pension programs and assesses the effect of these programs on general economic growth. He begins by discussing the economic rationale of public pensions, then analyzes the influence of economic and demographic variables on the cost of a pension program and the effects of public pension systems on aggregate levels of income and capital stock. Suggesting that Feldstein's social security wealth (SSW) variable overestimates the amount of wealth generated by public pensions, Dr. Nektarios constructs a new SSW variable and uses it to estimate the impact of the U.S. Old Age and Survivors Insurance (OASI) program on capital formation and economic growth in the U.S. economy. The results of his econometric analysis suggest that operation of the OASI program has reduced capital formation by 10 to 14 percent.

Dr. Nektarios holds a Ph.D. in economics from Temple University, where he was a research associate at the Institute for Social Economics.

Public Pensions, Capital Formation, and Economic Growth

Miltiadis Nektarios

Westview Press / Boulder, Colorado

To my parents,

Agamemnon and Alexandra Nektarios,

for their love and patience.

A Westview Replica Edition

Published in 1982 in the United States of America by
    Westview Press, Inc.
    5500 Central Avenue
    Boulder, Colorado
    Frederick A. Praeger, President and Publisher

Library of Congress Cataloging in Publication Data
Nektarios, Miltiadis
Public pensions, capital formation, and economic growth
    (A Westview Replica Edition)
    Bibliography: p.170
    Index: p.181
    1. Pension trusts--United States--Investments. 2. Old age pensions--
United States. 3. Saving and investment--United States. 4. Old age pensions.
I. Title. II. Series.
HD7106.U5N35 1982   331.25'2'0973   82-20224
ISBN 0-86531-936-7

Printed and bound in the United States of America

10 9 8 7 6 5 4 3 2 1

Contents

PART 3

THE IMPACT OF A PAY-AS-YOU-GO PENSION SYSTEM ON THE ECONOMY

Tables and Figures

Acknowledgments

This work, with minor changes, is my doctoral dissertation thesis which I submitted to the Department of Economics, Temple University, on December 1980.
I would like to express my deep appreciation to my dissertation committee chairman, Dr. George F. Rohrlich, for his guidance and assistance throughout this study. This preface is also an occasion for thanking him sincerely for having had the opportunity to work for and with him during the period of my graduate studies.
I am also indebted to the rest of my committee members, Dr. Benjamin Klotz and Dr. Michael Goetz, for their most helpful comments and suggestions.
Moreover, I would like to take this opportunity to thank Professor George E. Rejda of the Department of Economics of the University of Nebraska-Lincoln, for arousing my interest in the economics of social insurance. Also, I am indebted to Dr. Rejda as well as to Dr. H. Wayne Snider, Professor of Risk Management and former chairman of the Department of Risk and Insurance, Temple University, for the encouragement and help they gave me in the early years of my graduate studies.

1
General Introduction

Since the Second World War, public pension plans have played an increasingly important role in providing retirement income for older people in most industrial societies. The leading factor that led to the development of public pension systems is the failure of private intergenerational and intertemporal transfers to make adequate provision for old age.

Despite their size and importance public pension systems still receive surprisingly little attention in the economic literature. The principles and criteria by which public pension programs should be designed are largely unexplored. The economic effects of these programs are largely unanalyzed. This study is an attempt to contribute to the analysis of these issues.

More specifically, our study consists of three parts. In Part 1, we will develop the economic theory of public pensions. In Part 2, we will analyze the influence of the social and economic environment on the cost of public pensions. In Part 3, we will analyze the influence of public pensions on the economy.

In the first part of this study, we will try to develop the economic rationale of public pensions by using a normative analysis which takes explicitly into consideration the basic objectives that a pension system is supposed to satisfy. In this regard, much of the existing literature is far from satisfying in that analysts frequently stress only selected objectives of the pension system, while ignoring others. Old-age pensions in modern societies have come to be considered as a social institution whose main purpose is to provide, to all qualifying individuals during their retirement years, an income stream which is (1) continuous, (2) adequate, (3) constant in terms of purchasing power, and (4) capable of maintaining the socioeconomic position of the retired; these are the four basic objectives of, what we have called, dynamic pensions.

It will be shown that private arrangements cannot satisfy all four objectives because of market failures or because of the absence of certain insurance markets.

1

Our analysis will permit the derivation of the basic characteristics of a collective mechanism which is capable of providing dynamic pensions. It will be shown that the basic characteristics of this system may be explained either as the result of deviations from the duality conditions for economic efficiency or as attempts to compensate by other social institutions for market failures.

Admittedly, satisfaction of the basic objectives of a pension program is very important; however, it is equally important to pay close attention to the costs of the program. Therefore, in the second part of our study, we examine the feasibility of the "optimal" (in the sense of second-best) public pension system that we derived in Part 1; that is, we try to discover the range of the potential costs of such a program. To do that, we develop a mathematical model of the pension system and try to determine the influence of certain economic and demographic variables on the cost of the program.

On the other hand, the public pension program influences the aggregate levels of income and the capital stock through its effect on the ratio of aggregate saving to aggregate income. Certain studies have appeared in the economic literature in recent years that attempt to analyze this issue. The third part of this study focuses on evaluating the empirical and theoretical bases upon which the capital effects have been estimated and on improving them. It is suggested that the social security wealth variable which has been constructed by Martin Feldstein over-estimates the amount of wealth generated by the public pension system. A new social security wealth variable is constructed, and it is used to estimate the effect of the U.S. Old-Age and Survivors Insurance (OASI) program on capital formation and economic growth in the American economy. Our research shows that when this effect is estimated on the basis of single-equation consumption functions, the estimates are sensitive to the specification of the consumption function. We try to estimate the impact of the OASI program on capital formation by using a long-run economic model of the U.S. economy, which is estimated simultaneously. Moreover, this model serves as the basis for a simulation which is used to determine what the capital-labor ratio for the American economy would have been if the OASI program had not been established.

Part 1

The Economic Theory of Dynamic Old-Age Pensions

2
Introduction: Scope and Method

The study of social insurance in general, and old-age pensions in particular, is a new and underdeveloped area of economic research. The existing literature on the economics of old-age pensions consists of a number of articles that may be classified in two broad categories : first, theoretical works which attempt to explain the economic foundations of the collective arrangements that have appeared in modern industrial societies in order to provide economic security during one's retirement years; and second, empirical works which try to quantify the influence of pension systems on the overall economy, and vice versa. Our work in Part 1 will attempt to make a contribution to the former area of research.

A common problem with all economic theories of old-age pensions (see discussion in Chapter 5) is that they have not been able to advance a satisfactory explanation for the existence of public pension plans; this is due to the fact that these theories do not analyze explicitly the nature of the commodity whose provision they try to explain. Old-age pensions in modern industrial societies are not the same thing as annuities, the traditional response of private insurance markets to the need of individuals to provide for retirement income. Rather, old-age pensions in modern societies have come to be considered as a social institution whose main purpose is to provide, to all qualifying individuals during their retirement years, an income stream which is (1) continuous, (2) adequate (meaning close relationship to the preretirement standard of living), (3) constant in terms of purchasing power, and (4) capable of maintaining the socioeconomic position of the retired in relation to that of the active population. These four basic objectives of, what we have called, dynamic pensions will be analyzed in more detail later (see Chapter 4).

5

An economic analysis of public pensions must
justify the need for social intervention; that is, it
is necessary to analyze why members of a group seek a
collective solution to the problem of providing for old
age rather than to rely on private market arrangements.

The theory of social intervention for purposes of
micro-efficiency is built upon three bases: first, an
analysis of the formal characteristics of an efficient
economic system (Pareto optimality rules); second, a
specification of the conditions under which a decentralized market system with private ownership of productive resources will duplicate those characteristics (the
duality conditions); and third, an identification of
the situations in which, existing private markets do
not or cannot meet those conditions (market failures).

In Chapter 3 the private markets for old-age
pensions are examined within the framework of a competitive model which disregards uncertainty; that is, in
this model insurance policies against all conceivable
risks and uncertainties are available. The Pareto-
optimality conditions are derived, and an explicit list
of the duality conditions (required to sustain the
competitive optimum) is provided.

In Chapter 4, we discuss the assumptions behind
the duality conditions. It is shown that most of these
conditions are violated in actual life because of
market failures or because of the absence of certain
insurance markets. This analysis shows that, even if
we accept the efficiency of the competitive economy as
a valuable reference point, there remain important
reasons for government intervention in the supply of
old-age pensions.

In Chapter 5, we derive the basic characteristics
of the collective mechanism that provides pensions
which satisfy the four objectives mentioned above. It
is shown that the basic characteristics of this system
may be explained either as the result of deviations
from the competitive conditions or as attempts to
compensate by other social institutions for those
failures. Finally, our model of public pensions is
compared to the existing theories that have been
advanced to explain public pensions.

From a methodological point of view, the analytical framework outlined above falls within the domain
of welfare economics. However, the value of the
welfare economics theorems as a reference point in
explaining the role of the government in the provision
of old-age pensions may be questioned, and we need to
consider in more detail what is entailed. The fact
that the market outcome is inefficient or inequitable
does not mean that one can deduce that government
intervention will necessarily lead to an improvement.

It has to be shown that there exist policies that will
solve, or at least alleviate, the problem, and that the
government is both willing and able to implement these
policies; this is the essence of our discussion in
Chapters 4 and 5. In other words, the basic aim of
our normative analysis of Part 1 is to explore the
relationship between the objectives of dynamic pensions
and the policy recommendations to which these objectives lead.[1]

NOTES

    1. For a clear exposition of the methodology of
welfare economics, see Anthony B. Atkinson and Joseph
E. Stiglitz, Lectures on Public Economics (New York :
McGraw-Hill Book Co., 1980), Lectures 1 and 11.

3
Old-Age Pensions in a Perfectly Competitive Economy

Discussion of the perfect competitive model in this context serves two purposes: first, to demonstrate that an old-age pension system is redundant in such a framework; and second, to serve as a basis for comparisons with actual alternatives.

Most arguments in economic theory assume that there is no uncertainty in the world. For many problems, where risk and uncertainty are unimportant, this assumption presents no difficulty. However, discussing arrangements that provide economic security in old-age is inherently related to issues of risk and uncertainty; as a matter of fact these are the most important considerations.

Arrow has extended the traditional welfare theorems to cover risk and uncertainty.[1] This analysis of efficient resource allocation under uncertainty will be used here to show how old-age pensions may be provided in such an ideal environment. We will deal here only with technological or event uncertainty, where individuals are uncertain about exogenous events (although they might be certain about the terms on which they might make market exchanges; this is the so-called market uncertainty) such as resource endowments or productive opportunities or public policy.[2] Dealing with this type of uncertainty only permits us to use the traditional model of perfect markets in which all dealings take place costlessly at equilibrium prices.

In decision-making under uncertainty the individual chooses among acts, while Nature may metaphorically be said to "choose" among "states of the world". Suppose that there are I individuals whose endowments (points in the C-dimensional commodity space) will depend upon which one of S mutually exclusive "states of the world" obtains. Let Xics denote the quantity of commodity c accruing to individual I (i = 1, 2, ...I) if state s obtains (s = 1, 2,...S), and $\bar{X}$ics denotes the quantity of commodity c consumed by individual i if state s obtains.

Moreover, suppose that there are S . C competitive markets for "contingent claims" to commodities with prices $\bar{P}sc$, s = 1, 2,...S and c = 1, 2,...C. $\bar{P}sc$ is the price, to be paid irrevocably before it is known what state of the world obtains, for a claim to one unit of commodity c, to be delivered if, and only if, state s obtains. With such markets for contingent claims exchange takes place immediately, and deliveries take place after it is known what state obtains.

However, in the actual world, risk-bearing is not allocated by the sale of claims against specific commodities. Usually claims are expressed in terms of money; the amount depending on the state s which has actually occurred. Therefore, the analysis has to be modified to allow for the existence of money.

Let Fs be the price, in period 1, of one dollar payable in period t provided that state s occurs; this may be defined as a "basic insurance contract."[3] An insurance policy may be conceived of as a collection of such basic contracts. If we denote as Psc the price, in period t, of one unit of commodity c, given that state s has occurred, then it is :

$$\bar{P}sc = Psc \cdot Fs$$

Price Psc differs from price $\bar{P}sc$ in two respects: first, Psc refers to time t (future), while $\bar{P}sc$ refers to time 1 (present); and second, price Psc is a conditional price which will be paid only after state s has occurred, whereas price $\bar{P}sc$ must be paid in advance.

In this formulation, a claim to one unit of commodity c contingent upon state s may be acquired by purchasing it conditionally, that is, by promising to pay Psc dollars against delivery of one unit of c should s obtain, while purchasing simultaneously a claim to Psc dollars contingent on state s for a price Fs · Psc. The latter exchange would take place in one of the S markets for contingent claims, and after a state s has obtained, the former exchange would be implemented in one of the C commodity markets.[4]

For a "representative" individual the problem in a case of decision-making under conditions of uncertainty is to specify: (1) a set of acts; (2) a probability function expressing his beliefs Πs as to the likelihood of the different states of the world; (3) a consequence function showing outcomes under all combinations of acts and states; and (4) a preference-scaling or utility function defined over consequences. This framework is quite appropriate for an analysis of old-age pensions; the decision problem for the individual is to make arrangements to secure an income

stream for the retirement years. Ideally, this income
stream should be continuous, adequate, constant in
purchasing power, and capable of maintaining the individual's socioeconomic position (see Chapter 4).
These desirable characteristics represent, in essence,
amounts of income the individual will receive as a
result of the interactions of the decisions (or "acts")
he makes and the "states of the world," that actually
occur. Table 3.1 shows the amounts of income Y_{as},
that correspond to various acts $a = 1, 2, \ldots T$ and
various states $s = 1, 2, \ldots S$.

TABLE 3.1
Consequences of Alternative Acts and States

		States; $s = 1, 2, \ldots S$				Utility of Acts
		1	2	...	S	
Acts:	1	Y_{11}	Y_{12}	...	Y_{1S}	U_1
Insurance	2	Y_{21}	Y_{22}	...	Y_{2S}	U_2
Contracts						
For income	:	:	:		:	:
in Period a;	:	:	:		:	:
$a = 1, 2, \ldots T$	T	Y_{T1}	Y_{T2}		Y_{TS}	U_S
Probability of state S		Π_1	Π_2		Π_S	

    The acts shown in Table 3.1 represent insurance
contracts that will deliver a certain amount of income
in a specific point in the future provided that a
specific state takes place. In essence, those
insurance contracts are market processes that provide
a variety of ways for sharing risks among the decision-
making units.
    The states of nature shown in Table 3.1 need not
be restricted to physical descriptions of the world,
like injury, death, sickness, unemployment, and so on,
but may include different possible levels of future
incomes (in that case income will be known for each
possible state) or possible prices in future periods
(in that case insurance policies will pay different
amounts depending on actual prices in the future) or
possible changes in tastes.

The lower part of Table 3.1 shows the subjective probabilities, Πs, $s = 1, 2, \ldots S$, that each individual assigns to each state of the world.

The last column in Table 3.1 shows how an act is chosen. This takes place in two stages: first, "cardinal" utilities $U(Yas)$, $\forall a = 1, 2, \ldots T$; $s = 1, 2, \ldots S$, are assigned to each element of a specific row of the consequence matrix and the result is a preference-scaling function of all consequences associated with a specific act;[5] and second, the connection between the utility ordering of acts, Ua, $a = 1, 2, \ldots T$, and the preference-scaling of consequences is provided by the Von Newmann-Morgenstern "expected utility rule":

$$Ua = \sum_{s=1}^{S} \Pi s \cdot U(Yas), \qquad \forall a = 1, 2, \ldots T \qquad (2)$$

That is, the utility of each act is the mathematical expectation of the utilities of the associated consequences.

The budget constraint for the individual is:

$$\sum_{c=1}^{C} \cdot \sum_{s=1}^{S} \bar{P}sc \, (\bar{X}sc - Xsc)$$

which may be written as follows:

$$\sum_{c} \sum_{s} \bar{P}sc \; \bar{X}sc - \bar{Y}$$

where $\bar{Y}$ $(= \sum_{c} \sum_{s} \bar{P}sc \, Xsc)$ is the present (nonstochastic) market value of the individual's (stochastic) endowment. After state s occurs, and provided that act "a" had been chosen, the quantity $\bar{X}sc$ is available for the individual to consume. Then, it is $Yas = Psc \cdot \bar{X}sc$, $\forall a = 1, 2, \ldots T$; this is the way that the Yas values in Table 3.1 are derived.

The conditions for expected utility maximization subject to the budget constraint (3) are :

$$\frac{\Pi s}{\bar{P}_{s\lambda}} \frac{\partial U}{\partial Xs\lambda} = \frac{\Pi s}{\bar{P}_{\nu\mu}} \frac{\partial U}{\partial X\nu\lambda} \qquad (4)$$

where $s, v = 1, 2, \ldots S$ and $\lambda, \mu = 1, 2, \ldots C$

and
$$\frac{\partial^2 F}{\partial x_{sc}^2} > 0$$

where F is the Lagrangian function to be maximized. The latter condition requires that the preference-scaling functions U(Yas) are concave, which implies that the respective individuals must be risk-averse. Condition (4) implies that, at the equilibrium point, the ratio of contingent claim prices in the states s and v is equal to the ratio of the individual's expected marginal utilities in these states. This result is analogous to a well-known result in the theory of consumer demand under certainty.

In addition, we assume that the production possibility set is convex. Then, perfect competition in the markets for contingent claims and the markets for commodities will yield an equilibrium set of prices that can support an optimal allocation of resources under conditions of uncertainty. This will be an Arrow Optimum (or Pareto Optimum in terms of expected utility) if no other allocation exists under which expected utility is higher for at least one individual without being lower for any individual.[6]

We may now state explicitly the conditions on which the Arrow optimum is based; these conditions are:
1. Existence of C markets for the respective commodities.
2. Zero transaction costs.
3. Convexity in production.
4. Convexity in consumption.
5. Absence of externalities in consumption and production.
6. Absence of public goods.
7. Proper distribution of income.
8. Universal risk aversion.
9. Unanimous agreement on probabilities.
10. The utility of income is independent of the state that obtains (in order to construct the unique preference-scaling function of the consequences).
11. Existence of S markets for the respective contingent claims.

If the above conditions are satisfied, then the market clearing prices, $\bar{P}sc$ (from (4)), will permit decentralized contracting between pairs of persons; the resulting exchanges will reflect an optimal allocation of risk-bearing. But the amount of information needed to specify all of these contracts is awesome. Thus, it is natural to expect that contingent contracts could be traded through a financial inter-mediary, like an insurance company.[7]   Insurance

companies purchase insurance in one form (the usual
purchase is of bonds) and sell it in another; more
precisely, the purchase of a bond yielding one dollar
in period t is equivalent to a purchase of each of the
S contingent contracts.

The type of risk-sharing described in the preceding paragraph may be regarded as mutual insurance.
Indeed, it has been argued that all insurance is best
thought of as mutual.[8]   The contingent claims model
of insurance developed above may serve as a modern
expression of the principle of mutuality. This
principle is much broader than the "reserve principle"
which is the basis of all commercial insurance
business. It can be proven that the latter is a
special case of the former. Indeed, the basic difference between them is that when the expected aggregate
social loss, due to a certain hazard, is not determinable, then the reserve principle cannot work because
it is not possible in such a case to determine actuarial prices. Such cases arise in real life (1) when
the number of risks in a insurance pool is small, so
that the Law of Large Numbers cannot fully work; (2)
when, even with large numbers, risks are on average
correlated; and (3) when the assumptions of unanimous
agreement on probabilities (condition 9 above) and
state-independent utility (condition 10 above) are
violated.[9]

The analysis above permits us now to derive two
conclusions concerning the relative efficiency of
private or public arrangements in the provision of
economic security during one's retirement years.

First, we may conclude that in the ideal world of
the perfectly competitive contingent claims model
public provision of retirement income would not be
needed. In such a world uncertainty about future
incomes, or future prices, or varying lengths of retirement life, or future tastes, is not a problem;
corresponding contingent contracts for all those
"states" will be established and the market process
will guarantee the most efficient allocation of risk-
bearing. Indeed, in this ideal world compulsory
insurance for retirement income would be redundant,
because, assuming that compulsory insurance is sold at
competitive prices, an individual who wants more
insurance can buy more in the private sector, and if
he wants less he will sell the difference in the
private sector ("selling back" works as follows: life
insured loans are made for the market value of the
premiums; if the individual dies before retirement
there is no debt; if he retires, his pensions will
just pay off the loans[10]).

The second conclusion that we may derive from our analysis is that when, for whatever reason, it is not possible to determine the expected aggregate loss that might be caused by a certain hazard, then the traditional private insurance arrangements based on the reserve principle cannot provide an efficient allocation of risk-bearing. We will argue now, and will show more explicitly in the next two chapters, that the absence of most of contingent claims markets in the real world makes it very difficult, if not impossible, for individuals to collect information concerning future prices, incomes, tastes, etc.; hence, it is not possible to estimate a priori the expected aggregate amount of income for future pensions. If the traditional private insurance market, based on the reserve principle, cannot provide retirement income, various collective mechanisms, private or public, may be more efficient; this is the subject matter of the next two chapters.

NOTES

1. See Kenneth J. Arrow, "The Role of Securities in the Optimal Allocation of Risk-Bearing," Review of Economics and Statistics, Vol. 31, April 1964, pp. 91-96; and K.J. Arrow and R.C. Lind. "Uncertainty and the Evaluation of Public Investment Decision," American Economic Review, Vol. 60, No. 3, June 1970, pp. 364-378.
2. See J. Hirshleifer and John Riley, "The Analytics of Uncertainty and Information - An Expository Survey", Journal of Economic Literature, Vol. 17, No. 4, December 1979, pp. 1376-1977.
3. Since the states $(s = 1, 2,...S)$ form a partition, an unconditional claim to one "dollar"(one unit of "money") is equivalent to S contingent claims, one for each state of the world, and its price is equal to

$$\sum_{s=1}^{S} Fs = 1.$$

4. The significance of this modification is that it permits economizing on the number of markets; an optimum allocation can be obtained through S+C markets only instead of S·C markets.
5. For an informal presentation of the construction of a preference-scaling function see J. Hirshleifer and John Riley, "The Analytics of Uncertainty...", Ibid, pp. 1379-1382.

6. It should be noted that when subjective probabilities are not the same for all individuals then
Arrow optimality in a pure exchange model is equivalent
to maximizing a social welfare function, the implied
redistribution policy of which can be enforced ex post.
But the real importance of the Arrow optimality concept
is that in a model that combines pure exchange with
production this concept gives a basis for making a
choice of a point in the production set ex ante. See
J.H. Dreze, "Market Allocation Under Uncertainty"
European Economic Review, Vol. 2, No. 2, Winter 1970-
71, pp. 143-144.

7. Arrow's theory on contingent markets has been
reinterpreted for insurance by: W. Brainard and F.T.
Dolbear, "Social Risk and Financial Markets", American
Economic Review (Papers and Proceedings), Vol. 61, May
1971, pp. 360-370; R. Kihlstrom and M. Pauly, "The
Role of Insurance in the Allocation of Risk", American
Economic Review (Papers and Proceedings), Vol. 61, May
1971, pp. 371-379; and J.M. Marshall, "Insurance
Theory: Reserves Versus Mutuality", Western Economic
Journal, Vol. 12, December 1974, pp. 476-492. These
works do not take transactions costs into considerat-
ion. An attempt has been made to include such costs
in the contingent market theory of insurance in: J.M.
Marshall, "Insurance as a Market in Contingent Claims:
Structure and Performance", Bell Journal of Economics
and Management Science, Vol. 5, No. 2, Autumn 1974,
pp. 670-682.

8. See J.M. Marshall, "Insurance Theory...", Ibid.

9. While it is obvious why the first two reasons
result in non-actuarial (or market) prices for
insurance, the third reason requires some explanation.
If we relax either of the conditions 9 or 10, the
character of the equilibrium (see (4) above), is
upset; each individual takes market prices, adjusts
them by his own subjective probabilities, and then
finds his optimum by comparing state-dependent
marginal utilities of income. Since prices are not
actuarial, the reserves-based insurance is not an
efficient way of risk-sharing, but the validity of the
contingent claims model (which is based on nonactuari-
al market-clearing prices) is maintained. Indeed, the
only special case in which the two models of insurance
are the same is when aggregate loss is determinable.
In that case, provided that conditions 9 and 10 are
satisfied and assuming that aggregate income is always
divided in the same proportion (and also assuming that
all individuals have identical preferences and endowments of equal value, in order to guarantee Arrow
optimality), prices would be proportional to probabilities, that is, prices would be actuarial. In such
a case insurance on the reserves principle is

equivalent to an exchange in contingent claims. For
more details, see J.M. Marshall, "Insurance Theory...",
Ibid, pp. 479-481.

10. See D. Donaldson, "On the Optimal Mix of
Social Insurance Payments" in Old Age Income Assurance,
Compendium of Papers on Problems and Policy issues in
the Public and Private Pension System, Part III:
Public Programs, 90th Congress, 1st Session (Washington,
D.C.: Government Printing Office, 1967), page 134.

4
Collective Demand for Old-Age Pensions

An analysis that attempts to explain the various arrangements that provide economic security to the retired population will have to deal with two basic questions. First, it is necessary to ask what it is that persuades members of a group to seek a collective solution to the problem of providing for old age rather than to rely on individual action. Second, if collective desires are in some sense legitimized, then a choice must be made among the various kinds of collectivities that are available to provide such a good; they range from clubs and unions to trade associations and governments.

The answer to the first question will be given in this chapter. The conclusions reached here will point to the general answer to the second question mentioned above; the second question will be discussed in more detail in the next chapter.

Collective goods arise whenever some segment of the public collectively wants and is prepared to pay for a bundle of goods and services other than what the unhampered market will provide. A collective good thus requires that there be (1) an appreciable difference in either quantity or quality between it and the alternative the private market would produce, and (2) a viable demand for the difference. This general definition is quite adequate for our purposes.[1] There are important positive aspects in this definition; they determine the pluralistic nature of the sources of collective demands as arising from technical characteristics of particular goods, from market imperfections and failures, and from divergences between collective and individual values.

In the first section, we shall analyze the nature of a dynamic old-age pension. We will state explicitly a number of special characteristics that are indispensable to an old-age pension in a modern industrial society. In the second section, we will show that the existing private insurance markets fail to supply such a multidimensional commodity because

the actual performance of those markets falls far
below the ideal standards established by the perfectly
competitive contingent claims model of Chapter 3.

THE NATURE OF DEMAND FOR OLD-AGE PENSIONS

In modern industrial societies economic security
in old age can be attained if arrangements can be made
that will provide, during one's retirement years, an
income stream that has all of the following characteristics: first, the income stream must be continuous;
second, it must be adequate, that is, it must bear a
close relationship to the preretirement standard of
living; third, the income stream must maintain its
initial purchasing power during the retirement period;
and fourth, it must maintain the socioeconomic
position of the retired relative to that of the active
population, during the retirement period. This is a
realistic description of the composition of the
pension income made available to retirees in the major
industrial countries. The operation of all national
pension systems (the total of private and public plans)
is based, explicitly or implicitly, on the four basic
elements mentioned above; the major differences among
the various national pension systems lie on the
emphasis that they place on each of the four objectives.
The primary objective of a pension system is to
provide a continuous stream of income during one's
retirement years. As we will show in the next section,
efficient planning to satisfy this objective requires
knowledge of the length of retirement (and therefore
of working) life; that is, the risk here is that of
dying too soon or living too long.
The second most important objective of a pension
system is to provide an adequate amount of retirement
income, in the sense that the latter should bear a
close relationship to the retiree's preretirement
standard of living. As we will show in the next
section, efficient planning to satisfy this objective
requires knowledge of future levels of income.
Another major objective of a pension system is
to maintain the purchasing power of an initially
adequate amount of income, for all retirement years.
As we will show in the next section, efficient planning
to satisfy this objective requires knowledge of future
prices.
The final major objective of a pension system is
to maintain the relative socioeconomic position of the
retired in comparison to that of the active population.
As we will show in the next section, efficient
planning to satisfy this objective requires knowledge
of future tastes.

We may, therefore, observe that economic security in old age cannot be conceived of as a simple annuity like those sold in existing insurance markets; rather, it is a multidimensional commodity that can be provided only if a large number of uncertainties, concerning length of retirement life, future levels of income, future prices, and future tastes, can be dealt with in a satisfactory way at the planning stage.

Provision of such a multidimensional commodity would not be a problem in a world with a complete set of contingent claims markets like those of Chapter 3. All the uncertainties, and any other planning problems, could be dealt with by introducing basic contracts for the respective contingent claims and exchange of those contracts in the appropriate markets. However, in the real world most of the contingent claims markets are absent. The consequences of the absence of certain markets as well as the failures of existing ones, for the provision of economic security in old age, will be examined in the next section; it will be shown there that various supporting institutions have been developed to compensate for the deviations from the competitive conditions or for the absence of certain insurance markets.

SOURCES OF COLLECTIVE DEMAND FOR OLD-AGE PENSIONS

The interest in the competitive model that takes account of uncertainty, discussed in Chapter 3, stems partly from its presumed descriptive power and partly from its implications for economic efficiency. The ideal world of this model, however, can never be approximated by the actual world. Depending on the degree of deviation of the "actual" from the "ideal", society will, to some extent at least, recognize the gap, and nonmarket social institutions will arise attempting to bridge it.[2]

As far as provision of economic security in old age is concerned, observation of the actual world shows that people usually rely on some type of collective arrangement, e.g., group pension plans, and public pension systems, in order to provide for retirement income. Those collective arrangements, as opposed to individual provision, for old-age pensions will be explained here as arising out of (1) market imperfections, that is, failures of existing insurance markets and absence of most contingent claims markets, and (2) concern with the social environment, that is, market interferences which may take place even in a perfectly functioning market system, and which are part of and condition the environment of the society by rejecting market solutions to allocative problems

with respect to the distribution of income, or the
nature or quality of goods produced.

Market Imperfections

In Chapter 3 above we stated a list of conditions
which, if satisfied, would permit a private market
system to reach an efficient allocation of resources;
in such an ideal world individual, as opposed to
collective, provision for retirement income would be
feasible for everybody who would be willing to do so.
Even in this case, however, as we stated above and as
we are goind to discuss more extensively below, some
public provision of old-age pensions could be
justified on distributional grounds; but the essence
of our argument is that the collective arrangements
for retirement income that we observe in the actual
world are mainly due to the so-called market imperfections, that is, violations of some of the
conditions listed in Chapter 3.

Maximum efficiency, of course, is not a feasible
state of affairs in the real world, and it would not
be fair therefore to consider it as the basis for
judging the relative efficiency of actual markets.
A less strict standard will be used which states that
an efficient market presupposes (a) adequate information, (b) modest transaction costs, (c) timely
adjustment, and (d) sufficient competition.[3]   This
taxonomy will facilitate our analysis although the
taxonomy itself is not essential in our argument. We
will examine one by one the four requirements of
efficient markets, and we will show that the actually
observed collective arrangements that attempt to
provide retirement income, i.e., group pension plans
and public pension systems, are due to the fact that
the operation of the actual insurance markets
violates the four principles stated above; more
formally: the violation of those four principles
results in replacement of market determination by
nonmarket provision, or supplementation of markets
with ancillary public institutions.

Amount of information. In the first section of
this chapter we stated that in modern industrial
societies the demand for economic security in old age
is not satisfied by the mere possession of an annuity,
but it requires a dynamic pension that will provide,
for the retirement years, an income stream that will
be (1) continuous, (2) adequate, (3) constant in
terms of purchasing power, and (4) capable of
maintaining the individual's socioeconomic position.

Efficient planning for such a dynamic pension requires
some information about (1) the length of retirement
life, (2) future income, (3) future prices, and (4)
future tastes. There is an one-to-one correspondence
between the four types of required information and the
four goals of a dynamic pension.

In the ideal world of Chapter 3 the required
information would be made readily available in the
appropriate markets. But in the real world such
markets are absent; there are two reasons for that :
one is that forward contracts are more costly to
enforce than contemporaneous contracts; and the other
is that because of the many uncertainties about the
future, neither buyers nor sellers are willing to make
commitments which completely define their future
actions.[4]   The absence of markets for the various
types of information mentioned above leads to second-
best solutions. We will examine the implications of
the absence of those markets for the process of
individual decision-making for retirement income.

In the real world individuals face some uncertainty concerning the length of working life, and therefore, the length of retirement life; this type of
uncertainty makes it difficult for individuals to
attain the first goal of a dynamic pension, that is,
continuity of income during the retirement period.
The sources for uncertainty could be either a decline
in earning abilities sometime in the future (due to
failing health or declining skills), or a large
increase in the disutility associated with working, or
from a combination of them. Whatever the sources of
uncertainty, the implications are the same: early
retirement shortens the period of accumulation and
lengthens the period of retirement which has to be
financed out of accumulated savings.

Insurance against the risk associated with the
length of working life (that is, benefits would be
paid if the periods of working life and actual life
did not coincide) faces, however, serious problems of
adverse selection (that is, greater demand for coverage by those with higher expected benefits) and moral
hazard (that is, strong incentives to bring about the
event insured against). It is impossible for private
insurers to insure such risks.

Let us, then, try to evaluate the relative
efficiency of the various methods that have been
developed in practice by private and public insurance
systems in order to deal with those problems.

As far as the adverse selection problem is
concerned, it can be decreased or eliminated by
increasing the size of the insuring group. Insurance
companies are able to offer annuity policies that are
close to being actuarially fair for large - and

moderate-sized groups. However, they cannot offer such
policies to individuals or small groups because the
adverse selection problem would drive premiums to such
high levels that would make it impractical to offer
this type of insurance. Public pension systems can
eliminate completely this problem by requiring
compulsory coverage for the whole population.

The moral hazard problem is a more difficult one
because it is not clear when working life ends; this
is so for most cases, although it is clear in case of
death or permanent disability. In order to deal with
the infinite number of cases where it could not be
definitely decided if somebody has actually ended his
working life, social custom has established a specific
age, usually around the age of 65 years, as the end
of working life.[5]   Part of the problem remains,
however, as long as different options are available,
for example,early retirement.

It should be noted that the compulsory retirement
age solves the moral hazard problem of the financial
incentive to retire early. If such a retirement age
had not been legislated, many individuals would
continue their work and, therefore, they should not
qualify for insurance benefits because there would be
no decline in earnings. To deal with this problem,
public pension systems use an earnings test that
transfers an individual's income from the state of
nature where he does earn to one where he does not.
This is an essential element of insurance against
decline in earnings. Public pension systems are more
efficient than private ones in dealing with the
problems of collection of information needed to
administer the earnings test.

We may summarize our concludions in the
following proposition.

> PROPOSITION 1:   The attainment of the goal of a
> continuous income stream for all retirement years
> is made difficult because of the uncertainty
> associated with the length of working and
> retirement life. This type of uncertainty is
> basically an uninsurable exposure because of
> serious problems of adverse selection and moral
> hazard. Public insurance is justified only if it
> is possible to reduce or eliminate these problems.
> In fact, public pension systems are more effect-
> ive than private ones in eliminating the adverse
> selection problem by requiring compulsory
> coverage of the whole population. Private
> insurers cannot provide coverage for all
> individuals, unless those individuals belong to
> a group of at least moderate size.

The financial incentive to retire early is faced
equally well by both types of systems by
establishing a uniform retirement age. As far as
the earning test is concerned,public pension
systems are more efficient in collecting the
needed information.

Uncertainty about future income streams makes it
difficult for individuals to attain the second goal of
a dynamic pension, that is, to secure an adequate
amount of retirement income that will be close to the
individual's preretirement standard of living. This
type of uncertainty causes serious problems as far as
insurance coverage is concerned. Insurance policies
would pay different amounts depending on the income of
the insured person, but a moral hazard problem would
be present in this case because individual behavior
affects incomes. Consequently, a private insurer
would not be willing to sell a policy written for an
undefined amount of future (retirement) income. In
most cases it is not possible for the insurer, or even
the insured, to determine a priori a future (retirement)
level of income that will bear a certain relationship
to an individual's preretirement standard of living;
hence the moral hazard cannot be eliminated. For the
same reasons, the government cannot provide insurance
in this case.
   In practice, various policies have been developed
by private insurance markets or public pension systems
to deal with this problem.
   Private pension plans grant benefits that
generally fall into two broad categories. Most plans
are "defined benefit plans"; they offer pensions that
represent a fraction of the retired employee's average
salary multiplied by the number of years in work. An
employee's salary may be averaged over his entire
career or computed over a shorter period just before
retirement. On the other hand, some plans are
"defined contributions plans"; in this case a percentage of an employee's salary is set aside annually and
pensions depend upon the performance of the accumulated
pension fund. The former method, of course, is more
efficient in providing pensions that are directly
related to the preretirement standard of living; the
increasing use of this method by the private insurance
industry indicates that the industry has found an
effective way to deal with the problem of moral hazard
mentioned above.[6]   Similarly, public pensions,
especially those based on pay-as-you-go pension systems,
are related to past earnings, but the linkage is more
direct and more sophisticated than for private pensions.

The exact nature of this linkage is not important for this discussion.[7]
   There are two basic points that may be derived from the preceding discussion. First, a decision must be made about the percentage of the preretirement standard of living to be replaced by pensions during retirement. Once such a percentage has been determined, the next task is to determine the appropriate public-private pension mix that will meet this goal. There is a trade-off between public and private pension programs, because, as our discussion above showed, both types of programs are equally capable of replacing a certain percentage of preretirement income, keeping everything else constant.[8]
   We state our conclusions as follows.

   PROPOSITION 2: The attainment of the goal of adequate retirement income is made difficult because of the uncertainty associated with future incomes. This type of uncertainty represents an uninsurable exposure because of the problem of moral hazard. In practice, there are equally effective methods (earnings-related pensions) for both private and public pension systems to reduce or eliminate this problem; this is so if everything else is kept constant. The appropriate public-private pension mix, therefore, must be decided on the basis of the relative efficiency of the two systems in satisfying the other objectives of a dynamic pension.

   Undertainty about future prices makes it difficult for individuals to attain the third basic goal of a dynamic pension, namely the maintenance of the purchasing power, for all retirement years, of an initially adequate pension.
   Moreover, ignorance of future prices has an adverse effect on the process of accumulation during one's working life; a sustained period of inflation may reduce substantially the real value of the assets that an individual or a pension plan has accumulated to finance a retirement pension. Individuals are the least able to deal with this problem because they face an array of investment opportunities ranging from fixed yield-low risk assets to variable yield-high risk assets that require an amount of sophistication which is not possessed by the majority of the population. Private insurance plans try to deal with this problem by investing their reserves in assets which have expected returns that will hopefully offset increases in the inflation rate. If the offset is not complete, then additional funding is required (this

problem will be taken up again in Chapter 5 below). On
the other hand, public pension systems have been more
effective in dealing with the problem of revaluing past
earnings in order to eliminate the influence of
inflation; evidence shows that there are quite a few
successful methods that are currently employed by
public pension systems.[9]

As far as maintenance of the purchasing power of
a pension during the retirement period is concerned, it
has proved to be very difficult for private insurance,
operating on the principle of advance funding, to issue
annuities that adjust for changes in prices; of course,
the reason is the lack of knowledge about changes in
prices in the future. Even the few plans that offer
variable annuities have not been able to deal effect-
ively with the problem of inflation.

The same problem would be faced by public pension
systems which operate on the reserve principle. On
the other hand, pay-as-you-go pension systems are, by
design, very effective in adjusting pensions during
retirement for changes in the inflation rate.

All the problems mentioned above arise because of
the absence of markets for real annuities. If it were
felt that this problem alone is the main issue, then
the answer would be the issuance of indexed bonds by
the government rather than the development of a large
public pension system; having the system, however,
lessens the importance of the presence or absence of
such bonds.

We may state our conclusions as follows.

PROPOSITION 3: The absence of real bonds makes
it difficult for individuals to accumulate assets
before retirement, and also to maintain the
purchasing power of their pensions after retirement. Private pension plans have not been very
successful in dealing with those problems,
whereas, on the other hand, public pension
systems, and especially pay-as-you-go systems,
have been very effective in providing arrangements that maintain the purchasing power of
contributions as well as pensions.

Finally, it should be noted that in modern
industrial societies it is possible that, over a
number of years, the standard of living of the average
pensioner falls substantially below the standard of
living of the current average worker because of rapid
growth in the economy. Ideally, insurance policies
would take care of such a "change in tastes", but such
policies are not actually sold because the associated
moral hazard is too strong.

In practice, this problem could be remedied by adjusting pensions for changes in the growth rate of productivity; then the argument is the same as in the case of adjusting pensions for inflation.
We may state our conclusions as follows.

PROPOSITION 4: Uncertainty about future tastes makes it difficult for individuals to meet the goal of maintaining their socioeconomic position during retirement in relation to the respective position of the current average worker. Public pension plans are more effective than private ones in providing arrangements to do that.

Transaction costs. The second type of potential market imperfection to be examined here is the volume of transaction costs in the private insurance markets that provide old-age pensions. These markets give generally rise to two types of costs: the cost of providing the product, and the cost of convincing would-be purchasers to buy. The latter is our subject in this subsection; the former will be analyzed below.
The essential point is that in some cases high transaction costs inhere in a particular service and they may be considered as an externality that is not worth internalizing (e.g., metering costs for water consumption in an area of high population density); but when high transaction costs reflect the institutional arrangements of a market they are a potential additional source of collective concern.
Costs of writing insurance are likely to be quite different depending on the institutional arrangements. Both buyers and sellers of old-age pensions incur costs. Buyers' costs include filling out forms, loss of time, medical examinations, information costs, the trouble of paying premiums, and keeping records. Selling costs include commissions to salesmen, advertising, and the cost of acquiring information about the potential exposures; in addition, a supplier faces administrative costs like accounting, portfolio management, and investigating and paying claims.
Empirical evidence shows that there are economies of scale in the insurance market for old-age pensions. Indeed as we move from individual policies to group policies to public pension systems we may observe that buyers' costs decrease continually, costs for salesmen are eliminated, and economies of scale in administration costs may be fully exploited. In a pay-as-you-go pension system the latter type of costs is further decreased because there is no need for portfolio management. In the U.S. Old Age and Survivors

Insurance Program administrative costs run about two percent of contributions or benefit payments, which are both about the same size. This, of course, does not include the costs to employers, the self-employed, and the IRS in handling their sides of the financial transactions; most probably, total transaction costs are less than four percent of outgo. Also, international evidence shows that similar programs in other industrialized countries have administrative costs of about two to three percent of benefit payments.[10]

In contrast, 17 percent of total outgo of the life insurance industry in the United States, on the average for the last two decades, was for operating expenses. These numbers represent an averaging of much higher numbers for individual policies and much lower for group policies. For example, for eight leading companies expenses as percentage of premiums averaged six percent for group policies and twenty-seven percent for individual policies.[11]

Time-lags in market adjustment. This issue is discussed here basically for the purpose of completion of the overall analysis rather than because of the importance of this issue for insurance markets. Due to the nature of insurance the development of new products is not a terribly important issue; while there may be new types of policies introduced, these may often be due to changes in demand rather than inventions of previously unthought of policies.[12]

One of the usual criticisms of the relatively uniform public pension program is that it does not exhibit much variation to fit individual needs. But the importance of this problem is limited by three factors.[13] First, because of the considerable gains of pooling, even private markets offer mostly group policies which have limited individual variation. Second, in any case the private market continues to exist (but this helps only those that need more coverage). Third, a public pensions system might not be an optimal one, but a sensibly chosen public program may economize on decision making insofar as this is not reasonably well done by individuals.

Degree of competition. The assumption of perfect competition is based on the understanding that there is a large number of companies producing a certain good with rising average variable costs in the short term (rising average total costs for each firm in the long term). When, however, there are economies of scale in some sectors then one producing unit has the lowest feasible average costs and operates in an interval of production where average costs are decreasing.

There are two strong arguments that can be used
to show that public provision of old-age pensions
involves economies of scale. First, it was shown
above that the cost of administering the insurance
declines with every increase in the amount of
insurance written. This is not an argument, however,
for government takeover of all insurance lines.
Economies of scale in the provision of insurance occur
when the operations of insurance are fairly routine;
for example, in old-age pensions the operations do not
involve any difficulties in defining the rights of the
participants because it is a relatively easy matter to
determine who should get how much in benefits. When
definitions of insurance rights are not straightfor-
ward costs begin to rise beyond a scale of operations
that permits a number of companies to occupy the
field, and the case for state monopoly is much weaker.
      Second, even the costs of providing the product
are lower in the case of public provision of old-age
pensions. There are two reasons that this is so. On
the one hand, a public pensions program is able to
avoid the adverse selection problem because the
coverage of the whole population is compulsory. Hence,
the average premium charged will be lower than that
charged by private insurance firms where the adverse
selection problem is present (in that case companies
have to charge an average premium rate; for many low-
risk individuals this rate may be too high, so they
may choose not to insure. This, then, will drive
premiums further upward).
      On the other hand, in a compulsory program the
safety margin in the premium rate need not be as
large as for a private insurer, because in the former
case the whole population is pooled and therefore the
variance of the average benefit payment approaches
zero.
      We conclude that lower costs of production make
the price of old-age insurance lower in the compulsory
program than in the private market; hence,a compulsory
pension program would result in a real gain to society
(the issue of the excess burden of compulsion is
discussed below).
      We may state our conclusions as follows.

      PROPOSITION 5: A public pension system (either
      of the pay-as-you-go type, or fully funded) has
      lower transactions costs as well as production
      costs in comparison to a private insurance
      system that operates on the reserve principle.
      The operation of a public pension system,
      therefore, keeping everything else constant,
      will result in a real gain to society.

Concern With The Social Environment

Up to this point old-age pensions have been discussed in terms of market failure - failure due to either the absence or the imperfections of capital and insurance markets. This is the grand tradition of classical economics. But even perfectly functioning markets for all goods and services would not eliminate the desire for market interference. As far as provision of old-age pensions is concerned, complementary arrangements to private markets or alternatives to them may be sought because of concern with the distribution of income or because of paternalistic attitudes concerning the nature or quality of the product under consideration. We shall discuss both issues in turn.

Redistribution of income.   Some general remarks are in order first.

It has been argued that optimality, in a context of risk-sharing, includes much that appears to be motivated by distributional value judgments when looked at in a narrower context.[14]   On the other hand, it is noteworthy that virtually nowhere is there a system of subsidies that has as its aim simply an equalization of income.[15]   The essence of the former argument is that it is generally impossible to separate transfers, taxes, and insurance; most social insurance programs redistribute income by charging prices that are different from competitive prices; moreover, most government programs that are usually thought to be primarily redistributing income do this by providing some kind of insurance. For example, relief payments to the poor provide insurance against income loss for any reason. Programs for blindness, disability, and so on, are providing insurance for those born normal, and insurance for the parents of all children.[16]   Private philanthropy provides the same kind of insurance. Orphanages insure children against the loss of their parents.

Clearly, then, many social services have an insurance aspect. Any insurance scheme redistributes income ex post from the lucky to the unlucky. This is true of both private and public insurance schemes. But public insurance can be more redistributive ex post, as compared to private insurance, for either of two reasons. First, it could simply have a wider coverage than the private scheme, even though each is equally redistributive ex ante. Second, it could be more redistributive ex ante.[17]

We will take the first point first, and will relate our discussion from now on to old-age pensions.

Income redistribution in old-age insurance results
from the fact that this type of insurance is sold at
the same price to everyone; the reason, of course, is
that no information is available a priori to permit
differentiated pricing. This lack of individual prices
results in elimination of substitution effects; only
income effects remain after uniform pricing in both
compulsory pensions systems and private group pension
plans. The income effect in this case consists of
transfer of income away from good actuarial risks
(those who die soon after retirement) to bad actuarial
risks (those with the highest probabilities of living).
In this framework "good risks" would be those people
who have high mortality rates (e.g. those belonging
to certain races, low-income people, and people with
low education) and those people who enter the labor
force early in their lives. People with the opposite
characteristics are the "bad risks" who benefit from
the transfers.[18]

It should be noted that this intracohort redistribution of income is inherent in both compulsory
plans and group pension plans (of course, it is more
extensive in the former due to larger size) and
results from the uniform pricing practices in both
types of plans. This fact should not be confused with
the lower cost of production in the compulsory
pensions systems (resulting from economies of scale
in administration costs and lower pure premiums due
to better predictability of risks); this is a real
gain to economy and it increases total income, and
may not decrease the income of any individual at all.

The second reason that compulsory pensions
systems may be more redistributive ex post, in
cimparison to private plans, is that such compulsory
plans may be more redistributive ex ante. Indeed
casual inspection suggests that most governments run
many programs that are ex ante equalizing. Equalization ex ante implies a tenuous relationship between
the financing structure and the benefit structure of
a program. That is, the financing of such a program
is not related to those factors that give rise to an
event that would result in payment by the program.
Most government health-care and sickness-benefit
schemes are not financed in a way related to a
person's health but, rather, in relation to income.

As far as old-age pensions are concerned, the
question arises now if redistribution by means of
equalization ex ante is called for. To answer this
question we shall consider two cases : when there is
initially a "proper" distribution of income, and when
there is not.

A "proper" distribution of income is assigned an objective meaning here: that is, each economic unit (individual, family) has enough lifetime income to satisfy current consumption needs and also the need of saving for retirement. Such a situation could be attained, for example, if economic policies were successful in providing each individual not only with an employment opportunity but also with an "adequate" level of income during this individual's working life. Under such conditions, old-age pensions would be related to past earnings in a strictly proportional way and no need for redistribution ex ante would arise.

Observation of the real world, however, shows that the distribution of income does not conform to the objective standard stated above. Inadequate incomes during one's active life may be due to one or more of the following factors: (1) premature death of the family head, (2) injury and disease, (3) unemployment, (4) substandard wages, (5) rapid inflation, (6) natural disaster, (7) being a member of a "problem culture", and (8) personal factors. Moreover, it cannot always be assumed that people who are in this category are in some sense "at fault" or undeserving. Ideally, a set of social insurances and other institutions could be used to maintain one's income at an "adequate" level during one's working life. In a first-best world purchases of contingent contracts for such events would guarantee economic security. In a second best world the absence of most of those contracts and the existence of severe transactions costs make it very difficult for many individuals to buy old-age pensions or to accumulate enough wealth to provide for their needs during retirement. In this case, provided that people are risk averse, and if it is true that most people do buy insurance for old-age, disability, and so on, government transfers should (at least in part) be provided in the form of transfers to the old and the disabled.[19]

The discussion above points towards universal coverage of the whole population for old-age pensions and, also, provision of a minimum pension regardless of past income; moreover, any portion of an old-age pension that cannot be attributed to past contributions should be financed by a device that equalizes income ex ante, for example, general revenues.

We summarize our conclusions from this section as follows.

PROPOSITION 6: A compulsory pensions system
is characterized by three types of redistribution.
First, the "private-insurance type"; this
includes the type of transfers inherent in any
private pension scheme, that is, redistribution
ex post from the lucky to the unlucky. Second,
the "group-insurance type"; this refers to
redistribution from "good risks" to "bad risks"
which is the result of large pooling of unequal
risks charged uniform prices. And third, is the
"equalization-ex-ante type" of redistribution;
this is the so-called "social adequacy" element
of public pensions. The latter type of redistribution occurs from the active to the retired
population and it takes place whenever a portion
of a currently paid pension cannot be attributed,
on a quid pro quo basis, to past contributions.
Universal coverage of the population for old-age
pensions in combination with inadequate incomes
during the working lives of a significant portion
of the population require significant redistribution of the third kind.

Paternalism. The argument in this section is
that because of concern about the nature and quality
of the commodity "old-age pension" its provision
should be made in a collective manner. Often the
nature of a good or service is affected by who
provides it. If it is left to individuals, they will
not save enough to provide, for old-age pensions, for
reasons to be discussed presently. It becomes mandatory then that the government override individual
preferences concerning consumption and saving
decisions and compel individuals to save for their
retirement needs. This paternalistic attitude of
governments may be justified on several grounds.
The first argument has been largely advanced by
Musgrave.[20]   He argues that if there were no
social security it would be necessary, on humanitarian
grounds, to have a welfare program for older people
with no other means of support. Such a means-tested
program would induce low-income workers to avoid
accumulating assets because of the high implicit tax
rate of the means-test. This situation can be avoided
with a compulsory pension plan that requires everybody
to save for retirement.
     This argument rests on the existence of inter-
actions among individuals and has been advanced as
the sole theoretical foundation of compulsory old-age
systems. However, this hypothesis rests on two

crucial assumptions: first, that income levels before
retirement are sufficiently high, and second, that a
careful plan exists which has as an outcome a living
standard which falls to the level supported by general
welfare. Both of these assumptions do not seem reasonable when considered in combination.[21]

More convincing arguments about paternalistic
attitudes in the provision of old-age pensions can be
made on the basis of severe costs of information
required for efficient decision making. Insurance,
annuities, and compound interest are all hard concepts
for a large part of the population to understand and
use correctly. This could be remedied by educating
the public on these matters, but this would be more
costly than government provision of old-age pensions.
Moreover, many people may be ignorant or irrational,
and admit to their faults. This is a common sort of
phenomenon in everyday life. A great many people feel
that they manage their money better if they receive it
fortnightly, say, rather than yearly. This is a wish
for a little less than the maximum possible freedom
of choice. Also, choosing now a combination of
present consumption does not permit an adjustment in
the future because of learning by experience; this
weakens further the case for consumers' sovereignty
over time.

In addition, it is evident in most cases that
for most individuals the marginal rate of substitution
between present and future consumption is less than
one. Such time preferences may result in increased
spending for present consumption and not enough saving
for future needs.

Whatever the tack taken in explaining paternalism,
the main line of the arguments above is insufficient
savings. In all these cases individuals are considered
to be myopic and ignorant about the importance of an
adequate old-age pension for their own welfare. This
particular reasoning implies that government knows
better what the "true" preferences of the individuals
are; in the short run, revealed preferences will
certainly diverge from these true preferences; in
the long-run, however, the government may hope that
the individuals will learn that the restrictions on
their behavior were imposed for their own benefit;
eventually their revealed and true preferences could
become equal. The way that the government may impose
its preferences in this context is by requiring
compulsory savings by all.

Finally, government paternalism in the provision
of old-age pensions may be justified on the basis of
empirical evidence. Diamond[22] tests the hypothesis
whether the saving patterns of a sizeable fraction of

Americans seem to be sensible. He calculates that a
sensible 60 year old person (who plans to retire at 65,
has an accumulation period of 25 years, and wants an
annuity equal to two-thirds the level of annual income
less savings) should save one-fourth of his income, or
this person should have a wealth-earnings ratio at age
60 equal to 6.25. Taking into consideration various
factors (existence of public pensions, welfare, uncertainties about the future, etc.) this wealth-earnings
ratio could become equal to three. Diamond's empirical
estimates show that twenty-five to thirty percent of
American workers have wealth-earnings ratio somewhere
between 1 and 2. He argues that forcing individuals
who are saving rationally to save a little more has
little welfare cost by the usual envelope argument; on
the other hand, forcing those saving too little to
save more would have a large welfare gain, since the
envelope argument is not symmetric.

We conclude as follows.

> PROPOSITION 7: Theoretical analysis and
> empirical evidence show that individuals, if
> left to themselves, will not save enough to
> provide for their own retirement needs. Or, at
> least, this is true for a sizeable fraction of
> the population. Compulsory savings imposed by
> a paternalistic government could solve this
> problem.

Propositions 1 - 7 provide the justification for
collective provision for old-age pensions. That is,
it was shown that both public and private collective
arrangements (as opposed to individual arrangements)
are capable of providing old-age pensions. If some
of the objectives of dynamic pensions are compromised,
then private collective arrangements may be considered
as satisfactory in the provision of old-age pensions.
If, however, the four objectives of dynamic pensions
are not to be compromised, then public collective
arrangements are the appropriate ones for the provision
of old-age pensions. This comparison is undertaken
more explicitly in the following chapter.

NOTES

1. For a discussion of this definition as well
as comparisons to other definitions of collective
goods, see: P.O. Steiner, "Public Expenditure
Budgeting" in The Economics of Public Finance edited
by A.S. Blinder, R. Solow, et. al., Studies in
Government Finance (Washington, D.C.: Brookings
Institution, 1974), pp. 243-257.
2. For an analysis similar to ours but with
respect to medical care, see: K.J. Arrow, "Uncertainty
and the Welfare Economics of Medical Care", American
Economic Review, Vol. 53, No. 5, December 1963, pp.
941-973.
3. See P.O. Steiner, "Public Expenditure Budgeting", Ibid, p. 252.
4. See K.J. Arrow, "Limited Knowledge and
Economic Analysis", American Economic Review, Vol. 64,
No. 1, March 1974, p. 8.
5. For a theory that views mandatory retirement
as a social institution that goes beyond the requirements of the social security system, see E.P. Lazear,
"Why is There Mandatory Retirement?", Journal of
Political Economy, Vol. 87, No. 6, December 1979, pp.
1261-1284. It is argued that the age of mandatory
retirement should coincide with the social security
payment age because, otherwise, an efficiency loss
will result. Also, see Peter Diamond and J. Mirrlees,
"A Model of Social Insurance with Variable Retirement",
Journal of Public Economics, Vol. 10, 1978, pp. 295-
336, and Eytan Shenshinski, "A Model of Social
Security and Retirement Decisions" Journal of Public
Economics, Vol. 10, 1978, pp. 337-360.
6. Over the period 1955-1974 the proportion of
private pension plans using a "final-pay formula"
(the most favorable for the pensioner variety of
defined benefit formula) increased from 38 to 78 per-
cent. See: A Study of Industrial Retirement Plans
(New York: Bankers Trust Co., 1975), p. 27.
7. For a description of a method that would
establish an intertemporally equitable linkage of
past earnings and current pension benefits, see:
U.S. Department of Health, Education and Welfare,
Social Security Administration. A Framework for
Analyzing the Equity of the Social Security Benefit
Structure, by D.R. Leimer, R. Hoffman, and A. Frieden.
Studies in Income Distribution No. 6. (Washington
D.C.: Government Printing Office, January 1978).

8. In the American setting the negative impact of public pensions on the private pensions system has been analyzed by A.H. Munnell: "The Future of the U.S. Pension System, and D.E. Logue: "How Social Security May Undermine the Private Industrial Pension System". Both in Financing Social Security, edited by C.D. Campell, (American Enterprise Insitute, Washington, D.C., 1977). For a qualification of the analyses above see: G.E. Rejda and J.R. Schmidt, "The Impact of the Social Security Program on Private Pension Contributions", Journal of Risk and Insurance, Vol. 46, No. 4, December 1979, pp. 636-651.

9. See, for example, E.K. Kirkpatrick, "The Revaluation of Earnings Records in the Social Security Systems of Six Countries", International Social Security Review, Vol. 31, No. 3, 1978, pp. 293+.

10. For evidence for the United States use: Robert Myers, "Administrative Expenses of the Social Security Program", Social Security Bulletin, Vol. 32, No. 9, Sept. 1969, pp. 20-27. For international evidence, see Max Horlick, "Administrative Costs for Social Security Programs in Selected Countries", Social Security Bulletin, Vol. 39, No. 6, June 1976, Pages 31 and 56.

11. See Life Insurance Fact Book, Years 1960-1976, (New York: Institute of Life Insurance), See, also Ralph Nader, Testimony at Hearings Before the U.S. Senate, Subcommittee on Antitrust and Monopoly of the Committee of the Judiciary, 93rd Congress (Washington, D.C.: Government Printing Office, 1973), Table C, p. 18.

12. P. A. Diamond, "A Framework for Social Security Analysis", Journal of Public Economics Vol. 8, 1977, p. 297.

13. Ibid., p. 297. Also, for a very interesting discussion of lack of differentiation in insurance policies due to compulsory coverage (which is caused by adverse selection problems) see M. Spence, "Product Differentiation and Performance in Insurance Markets", Journal of Public Economics, Vol. 10, 1978, pp. 427-447.

14. K.J. Arrow, "Uncertainty and the Welfare Economics...", Ibid., p. 949.

15. There is a very wide division of opinion among economists on the issue of income equalization by means of income redistribution. This is an old problem, but for evidence of this disagreement among contemporary economists see : Income Redistribution, edited by C.D. Campbell, (Washington, D.C.: American Enterprise Institute, 1977).

16. See D. Donaldson, "On the Optimal Mix...", Ibid, p. 133.

17. See R. Layard, "On Measuring the Redistribution of Lifetime Income" in The Economics of Public Services, edited by M. Feldstein and R.P. Innan, International Economic Association Series, 1977, p. 55.

18. It has been shown that these characteristics reverse the progressivity of pension schemes. See: H. J. Aaron, "Demographic Effects on the Equity of Social Security Benefits" in The Economics of Public Services, Ibid, Chapter 7.

19. See D. Donaldson, "On the Optimal Mix...", Ibid, p. 135.

20. See R.A. Musgrave, "The Role of Social Insurance in an Overall Program for Social Welfare" in The American System of Social Insurance: Its Philosophy, Impact, and Future Development (New York: McGraw Hill, 1968), pp. 23-40.

21. See P.A. Diamond, "A Framework...", Ibid, p. 289.

22. Ibid, pp. 283-296. An earlier study, using several plausible assumptions concerning interest rates, replacement levels, inflation rates, etc., found that the average American worker should have a savings rate between 16 percent and 23 percent during his active life in order to maintain his standard of living during his retirement. years. The existence of the Social Security system (benefits as of 1969) reduces the required savings rate to between 7 percent and 13 percent. In both cases the required savings rates are far below the actual personal savings rate, which averaged 5.4 percent during the 1955 to 1969 period. See J.H. Schulz and G. Carrin, "The Role of Savings and Pension Systems in Maintaining Living Standards in Retirement", Journal of Human Resources, Vol. 7, No. 3, Summer 1972, pp. 343-365. For more recent evidence of inadequate savings see: M.G. Sobol, "Factors influencing Private Capital Accumulation on the Eve of Retirement", Review of Economics and Statistics, Vol. 61, No. 4, November 1979, pp. 585-593.

5
Old-Age Pensions in an Imperfect Economy

With reference to the U.S. Old-Age Survivors and Disability Insurance program (OASDI), it has been argued that

> the individual risk of losing income through retirement or disability or (for dependents) the death of the wage earner can be calculated by actuarial methods and is covered by OASDI in a way that corresponds crudely to all kinds of insurance - through the "miracle of large numbers". In contrast, uncertainty can also cause loss of income in its definition as the inalculable probability of cataclysms that afflict an entire society: war, massive economic depression, inflation... Coverage for uncertainty, however, was judged to lie outside the operation of the system as social insurance.[1]

It is our main argument that old-age pensions in their modern form (that is, dynamic pensions which attempt to provide an income stream which is (1) continuous, (2) adequate, (3) constant in terms of purchasing power, and (4) capable of maintaining the socioeconomic position of the retired person relative to the working population) have as their main function the provision of insurance against these types of uncertainties that prevent individuals from making efficient accumulation of assets for their retirement needs.

More specifically, we showed in Chapter 4 that the various types of uncertainties that are associated with the process of decision-making for retirement income must be dealt with in a collective manner that makes risk-sharing feasible; moreover, paternalistic attitudes and redistribution may be considered only within a collective framework. These premises of collective demand for old-age pensions are the positive elements within our normative analysis. The starting point of our normative analysis was the explicit statement of the objectives that pensions must satisfy. The purpose of our analysis has been to explore the relationship between the specified object-ives and the policy recommendations to which these objectives lead; moreover our analysis makes it possible to examine the way in which the recommendations vary with changing objectives.

With respect to the latter issue, our analysis in Chapter 4 has shown that if the four objectives of dynamic pensions are not to be compromised the appropriate collective mechanism for providing retire-ment income is a public pension system. If, on the other hand, some objectives are compromised, then private collective arrangements, e.g., group pension plans, may be used to provide retirement income. The simultaneous existence of both group pension plans and public pension systems indicates that in reality there is a trade-off among the various objectives.

In this chapter our aim will be to use the seven propositions of Chapter 4 to derive the basic characteristics of a public pension system that satisfies all four objectives of dynamic pensions; because of its latter capacity we will call this system a holistic one. The holistic model will be described in the following section, and it will be compared to other models of pension systems in the last section of this chapter.

A HOLISTIC MODEL OF DYNAMIC PENSIONS

We will derive first the basic characteristics of the holistic model and then we will discuss the appropriate methods for financing such a pension system.

Basic Characteristics

The objectives of dynamic pensions may be associated more explicitly with the reasons that were analyzed in the previous chapter as potential bases of collective demand for this commodity. More specifically, the theoretical bases of collective demand for dynamic pensions give rise to certain characteristics which, if put together, will form the holistic model; these characteristics represent, in essence, social institutions which replace or supplement market institutions in cases where private markets are absent or they do not function properly. In other words, our holistic model is a second-best model of pensions.

In Table 5.1 we relate the overall objectives of old-age pension systems to the bases of collective demand, and we derive the appropriate characteristics

TABLE 5.1
Elements of Dynamic Pension Systems

Objectives of Old-Age Pension Systems	Bases for Collective Demand	Derived Elements of Dynamic Pension Systems
1. Right to an Old-Age Pension.	Externalities based on Paternalism.	Universal Coverage
2. Continuity of Pension Income.	Uncertainty about length of working and retirement life.	Compulsory Coverage. Compulsory Retirement Age, Earnings (Retirement) Test.
3. Adequate Retirement Income from a Pension.	Uncertainty about future incomes. Distributional Considerations	Principle of intragenerational Equity: Earnings-related pensions without redistribution ex ante. Redistribution Ex-Ante: 1. Minimum pensions for those with no or inadequate earning histories. 2. If Budget constraint present, then progressive benefit structure.
4. Pension in Real Terms	Uncertainty about future prices.	Adjustment of Pensions during retirement for changes in the Price Index.

Table 5.1 (cont'd)
Elements of Dynamic Pension Systems

Objectives of Old-Age Pension Systems	Bases for Collective Demand	Derived Elements of Dynamic Pension Systems
5. Retired Maintain Relative Socioeconomic Position.	Uncertainty about future tastes.	Adjustment of Pensions during retirement for changes in the rate of productivity.
6. Efficient Financing		Forced Savings; Contributory finance.

Source: Propositions 1-7 in Chapter 4.

of a pension system that satisfies all four objectives of dynamic pensions.

The first characteristic of a system of dynamic pensions is universality of coverage; this characteristic is based on arguments about externalities based on distributional grounds (see discussion that led to Proposition 6, in Chapter 4). We may note that it has been proven to be a relatively easy matter in most industrial countries to extend public pension plans to provide coverage of the whole population, whereas it has been especially difficult for private pension plans to extend coverage among small-size employee groups as well as among workers with unstable employment histories, like part-time workers, women, nonwhites, low-earners, and the self-employed.[2]

A second group of characteristics of a system of dynamic pensions includes provisions that would require compulsory coverage of the total labor force, compulsory retirement age, and the existence of an earnings (retirement) test. These conditions are necessary if the pension system is to provide a continuous stream of income during retirement (see Proposition 1 in Chapter 4).

Another set of characteristics of a system of dynamic pensions includes the principle of intragenerational equity and the principle of redistribution ex-ante. The former would provide earnings-related pensions, without redistribution ex-ante, to all retirees whose past earnings histories result in a pension which is above a, socially determined, minimum amount (see Proposition 2 in Chapter 4). More specifically, the principle of intragenerational equity means that each member of the same generation is entitled to a pension that bears a certain relationship to preretirement earnings - the relationship being the same for all. The implication of this discussion is that an "adequate" pension can be determined only at the time of a person's initial retirement because it would then be easy to determine this person's past earning history; as we will show later it is very difficult to arrange contributions a priori in such a way that they will make possible a posteriori to provide an "adequate" pension.

As far as the principle of redistribution ex ante is concerned, it means that uniform minumum pensions should be provided to those without past earnings histories, or to those whose earnings histories are not enough to secure a minimum pension; financing of these minimum pensions should come out of general revenues (see Proposition 6 in Chapter 4).

We should note that the previous discussion says
nothing about redistribution ex post, which in this
case would imply that a means-test is required before
the receipt of a pension; as opposed to redistribution
ex-ante which implies that an individual has a right
to a pension regardless of past earnings or contributions.

The two principles discussed above are necessary
if the pension system is to provide an "adequate"
pension. Additional characteristics of the pension
system might arise if we assume that there are binding
budget constraints for the pension system. In such
cases some compromises must be made; possible compromises may take the form of (1) a lower level of
pensions for all, or (2) some type of equalization
ex-ante in the benefit formula (graduated pensions).

Another set of characteristics of a dynamic
pension system includes the provisions for adjustment
of pensions for changes in the inflation rate and the
rate of productivity of the economy. These two
conditions are necessary if the pension system is to
provide pensions which are constant in terms of
purchasing power, and capable of maintaining the
relative socioeconomic position of the retired
individual (see Propositions 3 and 4, in Chapter 4).

Financing Provisions

The appropriate method for financing a pension
system may be chosen on the basis of certain criteria.
A logical (but not the only) criterion is the degree
of satisfaction of the four basic objectives of a
dynamic pension.

We shall discuss briefly the three fundamental
approaches to financing the benefits under a pension
plan: (1) advance funding methods, that are designed
to accumulate assets throughout an individual's
career, (2) terminal funding methods, which set aside
at the date of retirement assets equal to the lump-sum
value of an individual's pension benefit, and (3) pay-
as-you-go financing methods, under which benefits are
paid out of current operating revenues as they fall
due.

Advance funding of pension plans is based on
three cost elements: the normal cost, the asset
target, and the supplemental cost.[3]   The "normal
cost" is equal to the actuarial value of benefits
allocated to each active plan member during the year.
This cost is estimated on the basis of two types of
assumptions: valuation assumption and projection
assumptions, that consider such factors as the number
of members of the plan who ultimately will be entitled

to pensions, length of benefit period, type of benefit
formula, administrative expenses, interest earned on
invested plan funds, etc. The "asset target" is
equal to the actuarial value of benefits allocated to
date for all active plan members plus the actuarial
value of benefits payable to nonactive members. Plan
assets are frequently less than this target for one or
more of the following reasons: past service benefits,
change of the funding method to a more conservative
one, divergence between the experience under the plan
and the valuation assumptions, and liberalization of
benefits (e.g. early retirement with full benefits,
or cost-of-living provisions). The "supplemental
cost" is required to bring assets up to the "asset
target" over a specified period of time.

In principle, therefore, advance funding may
satisfy all four objectives of a dynamic pension.
This is true, however, only if extra funding is
possible when the "asset target" exceeds plan
assets; experience shows that extra funding is
actually very difficult to achieve for two reasons:
first, in employer-financed plansemployers are not
willing to incur extra pension costs especially for
people who are not current employees, and second, in
public pension plans that operate on the reserve
principle or in private plans which are partially
financed by contributions from employees, extra
funding might be impossible because those who would
have to pay additional contributions might have
retired (if, for example, additional funding is
required for cost-of-living adjustments to current
retirees). It seems, then, that advance funding
cannot guarantee the provision of a dynamic pension
because the aggregate expected loss cannot be
determined a priori.

As far as terminal funding of pension plans is
concerned, it may yield an adequate pension at the
time of initial retirement because this type of
financing eliminates all uncertainties about future
incomes. Yet, considerable risks are left uninsured,
to wit, the risk of varying length of reitrement life,
and uncertainty about future prices and future
tastes. Hence, this type of financing cannot
guarantee the provision of a dynamic pension.

Finally, pay-as-you-go financing of pension
plans is, by design, the most effective way of
providing for a dynamic pension. All four objectives
of such a pension may be satisfied simultaneously,
as our previous discussion has shown.

It might be argued, however, that the superiority
of the pay-as-you-go method of financing may be due
to the fact that the criterion used to evaluate the

various methods was the degree of satisfaction of the
basic objectives of a dynamic pension. Other criteria
have been suggested. For example, it has been
proposed that pension plans should be actuarially
funded because (1) this would negate the saving loss
resulting from pay-as-you-go,[4]   and (2) it would
guarantee intergenerational equity (that is, successive generations would receive the same rate of return
on their contributions).[5]   We shall show that
there are no significant differences between pay-as-
you-go financing and full-funding during the period
of transition when the pension plans expand in
coverage and liberalize benefits; differences arise,
however, when a pension system has reached its
"maturity" stage, but they need not be viewed as
titling the balance against the pay-as-you-go method.
     During the transition period the distinctions
between pay-as-you-go and full-funding are complicated
by two considerations.[6]
     First, there is the so-called "blanketing-in"
problem, that is, the awarding of benefits to individuals whose past contributions are insufficient to
finance the benefits that they can expect to receive.
In the private sector, benefits based upon past
service credits must eventually be financed either
by borrowing, or by reducing the implicit rate of
return received by current contributions, or - if
the plan is directly managed by the employer-out of
current profits. Similarly, in public pension
systems blanketing-in creates underfinanced benefit
claims. To the extent that universality of coverage
and fixed replacement ratios are considered as
indispensable elements of social security, the
distinctions between pay-as-you-go and actuarial
funding become a matter of degree, rather than of the
mere existence, of underfinancing. Blanketing-in
then blurs the distinction between pay-as-you-go
social insurance and private reserve-funded pension
plans.
     Second, in terms of its impact on intergeneration-
al equity, blanketing-in must ultimately force a
future generation to accept a lower implicit rate of
return on their "contributions" to social security,
be these in the form of general taxes, social security
payroll taxes, or contributions to a reserve-funded
pension system. How the income transfers to blanketed-
in beneficiaries are financed simply reflects the
incidence and timing of the reduction. Blanketed-in
benefits must be covered either by higher general
taxes, or higher payroll taxes, or by deficit
financing. The first two methods of financing cause
the current generation to bear the lower rate of

return implicit in the combination of higher taxes
with no change in the ultimate benefits it will
receive. Deficit financing represents, in essence,
an intergenerational consumer loan, and then the
relevant issues are when that "loan" will be retired
by a reduction in some future generation's lifetime
income and whether the incidence of the "loan
redemption" will fall on current consumption or
current savings when it occurs. The deficit finance
model also applies, if underfinanced benefits are
paid from accumulated reserves, in the case of
actuarial funding.

During its "maturity" period, that is, when the
influence of the financing arrangements discussed in
the previous paragraph dissipates, a pension system
is freed to realize all of the benefits that have
been claimed for fully-funded schemes - but only in
the absence of the economic uncertainties we discussed in the previous chapter. As we have stated above,
fully-funded pension plans are not capable of
eliminating those uncertainties and therefore they
cannot satisfy the basic objectives of dynamic
pensions.

The discussion above leads to three conclusions.
First, the most appropriate way of financing a public
pension system is the pay-as-you-go method if the
four basic objectives of dynamic pensions are not to
be compromised. Second, the degree of funding a
pension program reflects past decisions as to whether
the transfers to blanketed-in members of the program
were to be negotiated as offsets to current
consumption or as offsets to current saving. The
choice between a funded system and pay-as-you-go,
therefore, is not an either-or decision to be
resolved on the basis of equity considerations.
Rather, the fundedness of the system is to be
determined passively on the basis of purely situation-
al criteria, insofar as the incidence of transfers on
current saving or consumption is made consistent with
the prevailing needs of general economic policies.
In this view, the operation of a pay-as-you-go pension
system is not incompatible with the existence of a
small fund.[7]   Third, in a public pension system
there is no need for special concern with "individual
equity", as this term is used in the insurance
business. There are two reasons for that: first,
it is very difficult to disentangle the effects of
the three types of redistribution that take place in
public pension systems (see Proposition 6, in Chapter
4) and, therefore, the results of the studies that
purport to calculate rates of return on that basis
are questionable;[8]   and second, public pension

plans offer dynamic pensions that are capable of
reducing not only the uncertainty about the length
of retirement life (which is the essence of annuities
offered by private insurers) but also the other types
of uncertainties mentioned in earlier chapters, and
since individuals are differentially subject to
uncertain contingencies there are interpersonal
variations in the implied rate of return on contributions.

Finally, our holistic model may give some useful
insights for the implementation of the forced savings
principle of dynamic pensions; that is, how individual
contributions can be collected to finance current
pensions. We stated earlier that an "adequate"
pension can be determined only at the time of initial
retirement because only at this point is the whole
past-earnings history available; amounts of past
contributions are not relevant for this calculation.
Rather, current contributions are set at such levels
that are sufficient to balance current pension
payments. This proposed disassociation of pension
benefits from contributions points to two directions:
first, there is no need for keeping separate individual records of past earnings because this type of
information may be taken from the central tax
authorities which always record income earned from
labor for each individual; and second, since contributions do not constitute, in our framework, a basis
for future pensions, there is no reason that only
earned income should be the appropriate taxable basis
for financing public pensions - that is, financing
could be done through the income tax (where all
income is taxable) and in this case a certain portion
(probably the same for all) of the individual income
tax could be designated for the public pension system.
This method of collection of contributions would not
only minimize collection and administration costs,
but would also reduce income tax evasion (because
future pensions would depend on reported earned
income).

COMPARISONS BETWEEN THE HOLISTIC MODEL AND OTHER
MODELS OF PUBLIC PENSIONS

The economic literature contains three general
theories of public pensions. The first approach views
public pension plans as tax-transfer mechanisms; in
this case attention is focused on the relative income
positions of workers and those retired in each period.
Paul Samuelson's seminal 1958 article gave rise to
this theory.[9]   The second approach, we will call
it the insurance approach, views public pension plans
as savings arrangements; in this case the emphasis is
on "individual equity" - the relation between an
individual's contributions to the plan over his
working lifetime and his expected benefits during
retirement.[10]   The third approach, the social
insurance approach, is a combination of the two
approaches mentioned above. Our holistic model
attempts to provide the economic foundations of the
social insurance approach to public pensions. We
will show that our model has a greater explanatory
power than the other two theories.
    The first test of the theories is their capacity
to explain the existence of public pension plans.
    According to the tax-transfer approach public
pensions exist because individual saving is impossible
or very costly; this is the result of an assumption,
made by Samuelson in his 1958 article, that there are
not storable goods (the logic of this assumption
lies, probably, in the fact that a substantial
proportion of people are unable to provide for their
old age). Then, Samuelson proved that the market
allocation of "consumption loans" among individuals
was not efficient. The suggested efficient allocation
was a "social contract" between successive generations,
whereby the currently active population finances the
pensions of the currently retired population. This
arrangement is efficient in a stationary economy;
however, in a growing economy the "social contract"
is efficient only when the growth rate of the economy
exceeds the market interest rate.[11]   Since the
latter requirement is not empirically relevant, the
very foundations of the tax-transfer approach are
questionable, and therefore, this theory cannot be
used to justify the existence of public pensions.
    The insurance approach, borrowed from the
private insurance business and being the oldest
approach, provided the first technical basis for
providing some economic security to large numbers of
individuals who would not be able otherwise to

provide for retirement income. Hence, public pensions may be justified as compulsory savings, based on paternalistic attitudes.

Our holistic model shows that public pensions in an industrial society are, in essence, a social institution which has as its main objective to shield individuals from the potentially adverse effects of economic uncertainty on their retirement decisions. Our analysis has shown that it is the existence of a large number of uncertainties that prevents individuals from making provision for retirement income that is (1) continuous, (2) adequate, (3) constant in purchasing power, and (4) capable of maintaining the socioeconomic position of the retired person. We would argue that our explanation of the existence of public pensions is broader and more valid than those offered by the other theories.

A second basis of comparison among the three theories is the empasis that each theory placed on the various objectives of public pensions.

Advocates of the tax-transfer approach usually emplasize the attainment of the four objectives of dynamic pensions. To do that they recommend financing of pensions out of general revenues; however, this type of financing neglects the forced-saving aspect of public pensions. Our holistic model, although it accepts the same objectives, maintains the forced-saving motive, because otherwise individuals would reduce the level of their savings (thinking that they get something for nothing) or they would retire earlier (if years of contributions did not matter in the calculation of pension benefits); in both cases the costs to society would be increased.

As far as the insurance approach is concerned, its empasis is usually placed on the forced-saving motive, which, in this case, implies full funding of pensions. Our analysis in previous sections, however, has shown that full funding is not always the most appropriate way for attaining the objectives of a dynamic pension.

A third basis for evaluating the three theories is their provisions for financing public pensions.

As it was mentioned above, the insurance approach is based on full-funding of pensions, to the detriment of the other objectives.

On the other hand, both the tax-transfer model and our holistic model finance pensions on a pay-as-you-go basis. This method of financing has been proven to be the most effective in satisfying the objectives of dynamic pensions. Moreover, our model recognizes that the degree of funding of a pension

system has to allow for the results of transfers in
the past to blanketed-in individuals.

Finally, the three theories may be compared with
respect to the issue of individual equity.

Obviously, this issue is very important for the
insurance approach because "individual equity" is a
necessary requirement of private insurance rate-
making.

Most proponents of the tax-transfer model reject
the concept of individual equity; instead, they
justify graduated pension benefits on distributional
grounds.

Our model has introduced the concept of intragenerational equity (earnings-related pensions without
redistribution ex ante) which would guarantee equal
treatment to all participants; this assumes that
general revenues will be used to finance the benefits
of those without past earnings histories. In the
presence of binding budget constraints, our model
would suggest graduated pension benefits.

NOTES

1. Discussion Report of R.A. Musgrave's paper:
"The Role of Social Insurance..." in The American
System of Social Insurance, Ibid., p. 45.

2. See J.H. Schulz, "Public Policy and the
Future Roles of Public and Private Pensions" in
Income Support for the Aged, edited by G.S. Tolley
and R.V. Burkhauser (Cambridge, Mass.: Ballinger
Publishing Co., 1977), p. 14.

3. This discussion is based on: H.E. Winklevoss
and Day N. McGill. Public Pension Plans: Standards
of Design, Funding, and Reporting (Homewood,
Illinois: Dow Jones-Irwin, 1979), Chapters 10, 11,
12.

4. See M. Feldstein, "Toward a Reform of Social
Security." The Public Interest, Vol. 40, Summer
1975, pp. 75-95. Feldstein's main concern is that
a fully-funded pension system could be used to
increase capital formation.

5. See J. Buchanan, "Social Insurance in the
United States: A Program in Search of an Explanation"
Journal of Law and Economics. Vol. 12, October 1969,
pp. 249-266: E.K. Browning, "Social Insurance and
Intergenerational Transfers". Journal of Law and
Economics, Vol. 16, October 1973, pp. 215-237.
For a criticism of Buchanan's approach see A.R. Prest,
"Comments on 'Social Insurance in a Growing Economy:

54

A Proposal for Radical Reform' ", National Tax Journal,
Vol. 22, No. 4, December 1969, pp. 554-556.
        6. See A.M. Pitts, "Social Security and Aging
Populations" in The Economic Consequences of Slowing
Population Growth, edited by T.J. Espenshade and W.J.
Serow (New York: Academic Press, 1978), pp. 188-189.
        7. It is remarkable that most current proposals
for increased funding of public pensions are not
based on arguments about the security of future
pensions;   instead, it has been argued that the extra
funds should be used to increase current national
savings and capital formation.   For a critique of
those proposals see: A. Asimakopoulos, The Nature of
Public Pension Plans: Intergenerational Equity,
Funding, and Saving, A study prepared for the Economic
Council of Canada (Hull, Quebec, Canada: Canadian
Government Publichsing Center, 1980), pp. 27-48.
        8. There are quite a few studies on the rate
of return to social security recipient's contributions,
based on American experience. See C.D. Campbell and
R.G. Campbell, "Cost-Benefit Ratios under the Federal
Old-Age Insurance Program", and J. Brittain, "The
Real Rate of Interest on Lifetime Contributions
toward Retirement under Social Security," both in Old-
Age Income Assurance, Part 3, Public Programs: A
Compendium of Papers on Problems and Policy Issues in
the Public and Private Pension System. 90th Congress,
1st Session (Washington, D.C.: Government Printing
Office, 1967), pp.72-84 and 109-132; Y-P Chen and
K.W. Chu, "Tax Benefit Ratios and Rates of Return
under OASI: 1974 Retirees and Entrants", Journal of
Risk and Insurance, Vol. 41, June 1974, pp. 189-206;
U.S. Department of Health, Education and Welfare,
Social Security Administration, Office of Research
and Statistics. Internal Rates of Return to Retired,
Worker-Only Beneficiaries Under Social Security,
1967-1970, by A. Freiden, D.R. Leimer, and R. Hoffman.
Studies in Income Distribution No. 5. (Washington D.
C.: Government Printing Office, October 1976).
R.M. Peterson, "Misconceptions and Missing Perspect-
ives of Our Social Security System (Actuarial
Anesthesia)", Transactions of the Society of
Actuaries, Vol. 11, No. 31, November 1959, pp. 812-
851; R.J. Myers, "Analysis of Whether the Young
Worker Receives His Money's Worth Under Social
Security" in President's Proposals for Revision in
the Social Security System, Hearings before the
Committee on Ways and Means on H.R. S710, 90th
Congress, 1st Session, 1967, Part 1, pp. 331-341,
(Washington, D.C.:   Government Printing Office,
1967); see also "The Value of Social Security

Protection in Relation to the Value of Social
Security Contributions", in the same volume, pp. 330-
331. For a more recent study see R.S. Kaplan, "A
Comparison of Rates of Return to Social Security
Retirees under Wage and Price Indexing," in Financing
Social Security, edited by C.D. Campbell, (American
Enterprise Institute, Washington D.C., 1977), pp.
119-144. For a similar study for Great Britain see
A.B. Atkinson, "National Superannuation: Redistri-
bution and Value for Money", Bulletin of the Oxford
University Institute of Economics and Statistics,
Vol. 32, No. 3, August 1970, pp. 171-185. For an
argument that the equity-efficiency trade-off in
social insurance programs is less important than the
protection-efficiency trade-off see: Martin
Feldstein, "Social Insurance" in Income Redistribution, edited by Colin D. Campbell (Washington. D.C.:
American Enterprise Institute, 1977), p. 75.

     9. See P.A. Samuelson, "An Exact Consumption-
Loan Model of Interest With or Without the Social
Contrivance of Money", Journal of Political Economy,
Vol. 66, No. 6, December 1958, p. 467-482. This
model was not intended to analyze social security
specifically, although it could be used for this
type of analysis. In this connection see: A. Lerner,
"Consumption-Loan Interest and Money" (and "Reply"
by P.A. Samuelson), Journal of Political Economy,
Vol. 67, No. 5, October 1959, pp. 512-525; W.H.
Meckling, "An Exact Consumption-Loan Model of
Interest: A Comment," Journal of Political Economy,
Vol. 68, No. 1, February 1960, pp. 72-76; P.A.
Samuelson, "Infinity, Unanimity, and Singularity:
A Reply", Journal of Political Economy, Vol. 68, No.
1, February 1960. pp. 76-84; A. Asimakopoulos, "The
Biological Interest Rate and the Social Utility
Function", American Economic Review, Vol. 57, No. 1,
March 1967, pp. 185-190; D. Cass and M. Yaari, "A
Re-examination of the Pure Consumption Loans Model",
Journal of Political Economy, Vol. 74, 1966, pp. 353-
367; A. Asimakopoulos and J.C. Weldon, "On the
Theory of Government Pension Plans." Canadian Journal
of Economics, Vol. 1, No. 4, November 1968, pp. 699-
717; and Idem "On Private Pensions in the Theory of
Pensions", Canadian Journal of Economics, Vol. 3,
No. 2, May 1970, pp. 223-237; H. Aaron, "The Social
Insurance Paradox." Canadian Journal of Economics
and Political Science, Vol. 32, No. 3, August 1966,
pp. 371-374; J.O. Blackburn, "The Social Insurance
Paradox: A Comment", Canadian Journal of Economics
and Political Science, Vol. 33, 1967, pp. 445-446;

K.V. Greene, "Toward a Positive Theory of Intergene-
rational Income Transfers", Public Finance, Vol. 29,
No. 3-4, 1974, pp. 306-323; J.C. Weldon, "On the
Theory of Intergenerational Transfers". Canadian
Journal of Economics. Vol. 9, No. 4, November 1976,
pp. 559-579.
    10. For the basic proponents of this approach
see citations in Note 5 above.
    11. For a detailed analysis and expansion of
Samuelson's 1958 model see: M. Kurz and M. Avrin,
"Current Issues of the U.S. Pension System".
Mimeograph. Prepared for the President's Commission
on Pension Policy, June 1979, pp. 135-148.

Part 2

The Influence of the Economy on a Pay-As-You-Go System of Pensions

6
An Economic-Demographic Model of the Pay-As-You-Go System

INTRODUCTION

A common criticism of pay-as-you-go systems of pensions is that such systems are, in the long-run, more costly than fully-funded pension systems. A basic fallacy in this argument is the failure to distinguish between projected costs and ultimate costs of a pension system. In the case of a fully-funded system, the two costs would be the same only if the assumptions used in the cost projection materialized; but in reality they never do, and, as our analysis in Part 1 showed, this means that some of the basic objectives of a dynamic pension will not be met.

Admittedly, satisfaction of the basic objectives of a pension program is very important; however it is equally important to pay close attention to the budget constraint, because exorbitant budgetary costs would reduce the political acceptability of the program. The usual policy response in such cases of binding budget constraints is the adoption of some type of trade-off between the benefits and costs of the program.

In this chapter we will examine the feasibility of the pay-as-you-go pension system developed in Part 1; that is, we will try to discover the range of the potential costs of such a system. In order to do that, we will develop a mathematical model of the pension system and will try to determine the influence of certain economic and demographic variables of the model on the cost of the program.

The economic-demographic model of this chapter will be used in the following chapter to simulate the U.S. Old-Age and Survivors Insurance program, and also to make a decomposition of the past cost of the program and some projections of its future cost.

THE MODEL

The essence of a pay-as-you-go pension system is a tax-transfer mechanism that redistributes income from the active to the retired population. Obviously, such a system may be analyzed within a short-run framework, provided that, for the time being, we neglect the economic effects of the system (that is, the effects of the pension system on capital formation and economic growth; we shall analyze these issues in Part 3 below).

Our mathematical model[1] focuses on the influence of the economic-demographic environment on the pay-as-you-go pension system; this environment is reflected in the inclusion of the following variables: degree of coverage of the labor force by the pension system, the ratio of the retired to the active population, the rate of inflation, the rate of unemployment, the productivity rate, and the mortality rate. Although we do not pretend to have established a completely deterministic model, we do hope to capture most of the effects that the economic and demographic environment exercise on the pay-as-you-go pension system.

The revenue side of a pay-as-you-go pension system involves a tax on wage income of the active population, and the transfer side involves a distribution of the tax revenue to the currently retired population. In Part 1 we suggested that the tax should be imposed on total income and not on wage income only; this suggestion was the result of our proposed disassociation of benefits from contributions. In our quantitative model below we will continue to assume such a disassociation between benefits and contributions, but we will assume that the tax is imposed on wage income. Given the observed constant long-run relationship between wage income and total income, our conclusions can be extended readily to apply to total income.

The basic economic units in our model are the "average worker" and the "average pensioner". The former earns the average wage for each year of his working life, and the latter receives the average pension for each year of his retirement life.

People enter the labor force at age A and they retire at attainment of age 65. The length of working life is m years. Retired people die at the rate δ per annum; deaths are concentrated at the

beginning of the year. Babies are born at the rate d
per annum. The complete demographic model is developed in Appendix A; here we will state, without proof,
some of the results obtained in this appendix.

At any year t the total labor force, L_t, is given
by the expression :

$$L_t = L_o \cdot d \cdot \frac{1}{n} \cdot e^{n(t-64)} \cdot (e^{nm} - 1) \qquad (1)$$

where L_o is the labor force at time zero, and n is the
growth rate of the labor force annually.

At any year t the retired population, R_t is given
by the expression:

$$R_t = L_o \cdot d \cdot \frac{1}{\delta + n} e^{-\delta} e^{n(t-65)} \qquad (2)$$

The pay-as-you-go pension system covers a certain
portion of the labor force each year. We denote this
coverage by the letter B_t, and it may change from year
to year as coverage expands; its maximum value would
be unity. Also, the unemployment rate for year t is
U_t.

Average earnings grow at the rate λ annually.
This is a nominal increase consisting of b percent
increase in prices and π percent increase in average
productivity; hence $\lambda = b + \pi$. The nominal average
wage for year t, w_t, is: $w_t = w_o \cdot e^{\lambda t}$, where w_o is
the wage at time zero.

The covered labor force is taxed every year at
the proportional tax rate σ_w which is imposed on wage
income only. If we call this tax a payroll tax, then
the total amount of payroll taxes collected in year
t is :

$$\sigma_w \cdot w_t \cdot B(1-U_t)L_t \qquad (3)$$

or $\quad \sigma_w \cdot w_o \cdot B(1-U_t)L_o \cdot d \cdot \frac{1}{n} \cdot e^{n(t-64)} \cdot$

$$(e^{nm} - 1) \cdot e^{\lambda t}$$

The total amount of payroll taxes is distributed
every year to the retired population. We have to
distinguish, here, between two groups of the retired.
First, is the group of the newly retired; that is,
those who are entitled to pensions for the first
time. We denote this group by R_1. It is :

$$R_1 = L_o \cdot d \cdot e^{-\delta} \cdot e^{n(t-65)} \tag{4}$$

We assume that each member of this group receives a pension that is equal to γ percent of the nominal average wage for year t. Hence, the total amount of pensions this group receives is:

$$\gamma \cdot w_o \cdot L_o \cdot d \cdot e^{(b+\pi)t} \cdot e^{-\delta} \cdot e^{n(t-65)} \tag{5}$$

Second, the rest of the retired in year t (that is, those who were already retired for more than one year) have their pensions adjusted for either inflation or growth of average earnings. We shall consider both cases in turn.

Price-Indexed Pensions

The group of the retired who have their pensions adjusted for inflation is equal to $R_t - R_1$. From (2) and (4) we derive that:

$$R_t - R_1 = L_o \cdot d \cdot \left(\frac{1}{\delta + n} - 1\right) \cdot e^{-\delta} \cdot e^{n(t-65)} \tag{6}$$

The total amount of pensions for this group is:

$$(R_t - R_1) \cdot \gamma \cdot w_o \cdot e^{bt}$$

or $\quad L_o \cdot d \cdot \left(\frac{1}{\delta + n} - 1\right) \gamma \cdot w_o \cdot e^{bt} \cdot e^{n(t-65)} e^{-\delta} \tag{7}$

Hence, total pension payments in year t for the newly retired, R_1, as well as for the already retired, $R_t - R_1$, are derived by summing up (5) and (7).

The solvency condition for the pay-as-you-go pension system requires that, for each year t, the total inflow of tax revenues should be equal to the total outflow of benefit payments. By setting (3) equal to the sum of (5) and (7) and solving for σ_w, we can derive the payroll tax, σ_w, as a function of the other variables in the model.

Hence, we have for a price-indexed pension system:

$$\sigma_w = \frac{\gamma}{B(1-U)} \left(\frac{R_1}{L_t} + e^{-\pi t} \cdot \frac{R_t - R_1}{L_t} \right) \qquad (8)$$

or

$$\sigma_w = \frac{\gamma}{B(1-U)} \left(\frac{n \cdot e^{-\delta} \cdot e^{-n}}{e^{nm} - 1} + e^{-\pi t} \cdot \right.$$

$$\left. \cdot \frac{(n - n\,(\delta+n)) \cdot e^{-(\delta+n)}}{(\delta+n)\,(e^{nm} - 1)} \right) \qquad (9)$$

or

$$\sigma_w = \frac{\gamma}{B(1-U)} \left(E\,(n,\,\delta,\,m) + e^{-\pi t} \cdot \Lambda\,(n,\delta,m) \right) \qquad (10)$$

where:

$$E = \frac{R_1}{L_t} = \frac{n \cdot e^{-\delta} \cdot e^{-n}}{e^{nm} - 1}$$

and

$$\Lambda = \frac{R_t - R_1}{L_t} = \frac{n\,(1 - (\delta+n)\,)\,e^{-(\delta+n)}}{(\delta + n)\,(e^{nm} - 1)}$$

Reserving further analysis for the next chapter, we may state here that it is apparent from (10) that the payroll tax increases with increases in γ, U, E, Λ and decreases when B and π increase.

Wage-Indexed Pensions

In a wage-indexed pension system the pensions of the newly retired are determined as previously, and expression (5) shows the total amount of pensions for this group. However, the pensions of the already retired people are adjusted for increases in the nominal average wage in order to maintain a constant relationship over time between the economic status of the retired and that of the active workers.

Hence, the total amount of pension payments, for year t, to the newly retired as well as to the already retired may be given by the following expression :

$$R_t \cdot \gamma \cdot w_o \cdot e^{(b+\pi) t} \qquad (11)$$

The solvency condition requires equality of inflows and outflows. Hence, by equating (3) to (11) and solving for σ_{ww}, the payroll tax for the wage-indexed system, we obtain:

$$\sigma_{ww} = \frac{\gamma}{B(1 - U)} \cdot \frac{R_t}{L_t}$$

or

$$\sigma_{ww} = \frac{\gamma}{B(1 - U)} \cdot \frac{n \cdot e^{-(\delta+n)}}{(\delta + n) \cdot (e^{nm} - 1)} \qquad (12)$$

or

$$\sigma_{ww} = \frac{\gamma}{B(1 - U)} \cdot Z(n, \delta, m) \qquad (13)$$

where

$$Z = \frac{R_t}{L_t} = \frac{n \cdot e^{-\delta} \cdot e^{-n}}{(\delta+n) \cdot (e^{nm} - 1)}$$

The Growth Rate of the Payroll Tax

So far we have analyzed annual payroll taxes. It is important to establish a range of the potential magnitude of the payroll taxes required to finance a pay-as-you-go pension system under a wide range of assumptions concerning various economic and demographic variables that effect the cost of such a pension system.

Equally important, however, is to determine the cumulative impact of those variables over a long period of time. Such an analysis would make it possible to distinguish these variables which have had the greatest impact on the cost of the pension system over a period of years. Recognition of these variables is important for policy purposes. In addition, such an intertemporal analysis will permit extrapolation of costs into the future.

Continuing the discussion of our economic-demographic model of the pay-as-you-go pension system developed in the previous section, we will try, first, to develop the theoretical structure that will permit us to determine the influence of each economic or demographic variable on the growth rate of the payroll tax over a period of time. Such a general theoretical formulation may be given concrete empirical content by adopting a specific structure for a pay-as-you-go pension system; that is, by assigning specific values to the various economic and demographic variables of the model. This will be done in the next chapter.

We will consider first a price-indexed pay-as-you-go pension system. In order to derive the rate of growth of the payroll tax, we will take the logarithmic derivate of equation (9) with respect to time.

For our purposes here equation (9) may be written as follows:

$$\sigma_w = \frac{Y \cdot n}{(\delta + n) \cdot B \cdot (1 - U)} \cdot \frac{e^{-\pi t} \cdot e^{-(\delta + n)}}{e^{nm} - 1} \cdot$$

$$\cdot \; (\; 1 + (\delta+n) \; (e^{\pi t} - 1) \;)$$

Taking the logarithmic derivative of the function above and after simplifying we find that the growth rate of the payroll tax, $\dot{\sigma}_w$, is related to the rates of change of the economic and demographic variables of the model in the way shown below.

$$\dot{\sigma}_w = \dot{Y} - \dot{B} + \frac{1}{1 - U} \; \frac{dU}{dt} +$$

$$+ \; (\; \frac{1}{n} - \frac{1}{\delta+n} - 1 - \frac{m \; e^{nm}}{e^{nm} - 1} + \frac{e^{\pi t} - 1}{1+(\delta+n) \; (e^{\pi t}-1)}) \; \frac{dn}{dt} +$$

$$+ \; (\; - \frac{1}{\delta+n} - 1 + \frac{e^{\pi t} - 1}{1+(\delta+n) \; (e^{\pi t}-1)}) \; \frac{d\delta}{dt} +$$

$$(14)$$

$$+ \; (\; \frac{(\delta+n) \cdot t \cdot e^{\pi t}}{1+(\delta+n) \; (e^{\pi t} - 1)} - t) \; \frac{d\pi}{dt} - \frac{n \; e^{nm}}{e^{nm}-1} \; \frac{dm}{dt}$$

Working as in the previous case, but now taking the logarithmic derivative of equation (12) with respect to time t, we can determine the growth rate of payroll tax for a wage-indexed pension system, $\dot{\sigma}_{ww}$.

It is:

$$\dot{\sigma}_{ww} = \dot{\gamma} - \dot{B} + \frac{1}{1 - U} \cdot \frac{dU}{dt} +$$

$$+ \left(\frac{1}{n} - \frac{1}{\delta+n} - 1 - \frac{m \cdot e^{nm}}{e^{nm} - 1} \right) \frac{dn}{dt} +$$

$$+ \left(- \frac{1}{\delta+n} - 1 \right) \frac{d\delta}{dt} - \frac{n \, e^{nm}}{e^{nm} - 1} \cdot \frac{dm}{dt}$$

(15)

Equations (14) and (15) show how the growth rate of the payroll tax is affected by changes that take place, over a period of time, in the economy or in the demographic structure of the population. Moreover, the two equations make it possible to determine the relative importance of the factors that affect the growth rate; such a decomposition of the growth rate of the payroll tax is possible if information about the individual variables is available. An empirical analysis, on the basis of the conclusions reached here, will be undertaken in the next chapter.

NOTES

1. For another mathematical approach see : Richard D. Young and Gaston V. Rimlinger, "Mathematical Approaches to the Macroeconomics and Planning of Old-Age Pensions Systems" in Old-Age Income Assurance, Part III: Public Programs, Joint Economic Committee, 90th Congress, 1st Session, (Washington, D.C.: Government Printing Office, December 1967), pp. 137-155. More recently, several attempts have been made to include demographic variables in economic models of public pension systems; in this connection see: P.A. Samuelson, "The Optimum Growth Rate for Population", and "Optimum Social Security in a Life-Cycle Growth Model", International Economic Review, Vol. 16, No. 3, October 1975, pp. 531-537 and 539-544, respectively; Alan V. Deardorff, "The Optimum Growth Rate for Population: Comment" International Economic Review, Vol. 17, No. 2, June 1976, pp. 510-516; P.A. Samuelson, "The Optimum

Growth Rate for Population: Agreement and Evaluations"
International Economic Review, Vol. 17, No. 2, June
1976, pp. 516-525; Bernard Praag and Guy Poeth, "The
Introduction of an Old-Age Pension in a Growing
Economy" Journal of Public Economics, Vol. 4, 1975,
pp. 87-100; and B.W. Arthur and G. McNicoll,
"Samuelson, Population, and Intergenerational
Transfers" International Economic Review, Vol. 19,
No. 1, February 1978, pp. 241-246.

7
Empirical Evidence of the Influence of the Economy on the U.S. OASI Program

In this chapter we will undertake an empirical analysis of the U.S. Old-Age and Survivors (OASI) Program; this analysis will be based on the conclusions reached in Chapter 6. More specifically, in the first section we will employ equations (10) and (13) of Chapter 6 to make a few simulations of the cost of the OASI program under alternatives assumptions about certain economic and demographic variables.[1] In the second section, we will employ equations (14) and (15) of Chapter 6 to decompose the cost of the OASI program for the period 1950-1978; this decomposition will highlight those factors that played an important role in the formation of the cost of the program in the past, and it might also give some indication of the evolution of the cost of the program in the future.

SIMULATIONS OF THE OASI PROGRAM

The U.S. OASI program may be considered as a good approximation of a price-indexed pay-as-you-go pension system as that developed in the previous chapter. The OASI program was started in 1935 on the principle of reserve funding. By 1939, however, the policy of building large reserves was partially abandoned. Starting with the 1938 Advisory Council, all subsequent Advisory Councils suggested that the system operate on a pay-as-you-go basis provided that a "contingency reserve" was maintained every year. The contingency reserve had the purpose of providing for continuity of payment if Congress failed to act quickly to appropriate additional funds when current tax receipts fell sharply.[2] There was a silent agreement that the contingency reserve should be equal to one year's outlay; however, this principle became effective only in the mid-1960s,[3] and has been, more or less, maintained thereafter. Also, price-indexing of pensions started only in 1975.

69

The comments above should be kept in mind when the calculations below are evaluated, because our simulations of the OASI program are based on the assumption that a complete price-indexed (or wage-indexed) pay-as-you-go pension system, like OASI, has been operating since 1950.

Equation (10) of Chapter 6 may be used to explain the actual performance of the U.S. OASI program over the period 1950-1978. This equation describes the relationship between the payroll tax and the various economic and demographic variables that determine its magnitude. Columns (2)-(7) and (10) of Table 7.1 show the values, for selected years, of the economic and demographic variables that are included in the right-hand side of equation (10). A brief description of those variables follows; a more accurate description and the sources of those variables are given in Appendix B.

Column (2) shows the "replacement rate", γ, which is a measure of the relationship between the average annual pension, for year t, of the "average retiree" and the average annual taxable earnings for the current "average worker". Column (3) shows the degree of pension coverage of the civilian labor force by the OASI program, for year t. Column (4) is the portion of the labor force which is not unemployed. Column (5) shows the annual values of variable E which is the number of the newly retired people divided by the civilian labor force. Column (6) shows the annual values of variable Λ which is the number of the already retired people, for year t, divided by the civilian labor force for the same year. Variable π, in column (7), shows the growth rate of productivity for the respective year. Finally, column (10) shows the "dependency ratio" for the respective year, that is, the ratio of the total number of retired people to the civilian labor force.

Columns (8) and (11) - (13) show four simulations of the cost of the OASI program under different assumptions; the simulated values of the payroll tax rate are compared to the actual payroll tax rates for the OASI program, in column (9).

The simulated values of the payroll tax reported in column (8) are calculated on the basis of equation (10), that is, we assumed that the OASI program has always operated as a price-indexed pay-as-you-go pension system. Comparison of columns (8) and (9) shows that the simulated values are, for most years, higher than the actual values of the payroll tax.

TABLE 7.1
Simulations of the OASI Program

(1)	(2)	(3)	(4)	(5)	(6)	(7)	(8)	(9)	(10)	(11)	(12)	(13)
Year	Y	B	1 - U	E	Λ	π	σ_w	ACT	Z	σ_{ww}	σ_w (B=1)	σ_n
1950	.225	.59	.947	.009	.047	.060	2.16	3.00	.056	2.27	1.27	1.72
1955	.244	.79	.956	.014	.107	.040	3.79	4.00	.121	3.93	2.99	3.04
1960	.247	.80	.945	.014	.188	.010	6.56	5.50	.202	6.62	5.24	5.12
1965	.258	.84	.955	.016	.240	.034	8.00	6.75	.256	8.27	6.73	5.71
1970	.251	.83	.951	.016	.268	.001	9.05	7.30	.284	9.06	7.51	7.07
1971	.275	.82	.941	.016	.272	.031	10.00	8.10	.288	10.30	8.20	7.63
1972	.308	.83	.944	.017	.274	.036	11.09	8.10	.291	11.48	9.21	8.69
1973	.282	.85	.951	.017	.279	.017	10.20	8.60	.296	10.36	8.67	8.34
1974	.286	.82	.944	.015	.280	-.031	11.27	8.75	.295	10.95	9.24	9.62
1975	.300	.81	.915	.016	.282	.019	11.92	8.75	.299	12.13	9.65	10.08
1976	.304	.84	.923	.015	.284	.035	11.36	8.75	.299	11.75	9.54	9.56
1977	.280	.84	.930	.016	.283	.013	10.59	8.75	.299	10.75	8.89	9.46
1978	.279	.86	.940	.014	.281	.006	10.17	8.75	.295	10.23	8.74	9.17

Note : For explanations of symbols see text. Columns (8),(9) and (11-13) are percentages.

Most of the discrepancy may be due to the factors
mentioned earlier. In addition, the method of
estimation we used ("average" workers and pensioners,
etc.), errors in data, and political factors in
decision-making for payroll taxes and pension
benefits may account for the rest of the observed
differences between estimated and actual payroll tax
rates.

In any case, our basic objective in this section
was to use the mathematical model built in the
previous chapter to test the sensitivity of the
pension system to changes in the various economic
and demographic variables of the model. We believe
that the model can serve this purpose very well.

As a first extension of the analysis above, we
shall use equation (13) to estimate the costs of a
pay-as-you-go pension system that offers wage-
indexed pensions. Column (11) shows the simulated
values of the annual payroll tax rates for a wage-
indexed pension system, σ_{ww}. By comparing columns
(8) and (11) we may observe that when, in a
certain year, the increase in nominal wages exceeds
the increase in prices, then the wage-indexed pension
system is more costly than the price-indexed system,
keeping everything else constant; on the other hand,
when the growth rate of productivity for a certain
year is negative (e.g., year 1974 in Table 7.1), then
the previous conclusion is reversed.

A second extension of the analysis above could
be made on the assumption that the OASI program
covers the total civilian labor force; that is, B
becomes equal to 1 for all years. If this had been
the case, and keeping everything else constant, the
OASI program would have had substantially lower
payroll tax rates. Of course, the validity of this
argument will be partially reduced if we take into
consideration the fact that the expansion in the
coverage of the program will result in the long-run
in more pension entitlements. The simulated payroll
tax rates based on the assumption B = 1, σ_w (B = 1),
are shown in column (12) of Table 7.1. We may
argue, therefore, that one of the possible ways to
reduce the current payroll taxes of the OASI program
is to extend the coverage of the program.[4]

Finally, a simulation of the OASI program may be
made on the assumption that the program operates
according to the benefit and financing requirements
of the holistic model of Part 1 (that is, the payroll
tax is imposed on total, not "taxable", earnings and
pensions are related to current average total
earnings). Column (13) shows that in such a case

the required payroll tax rates, σ_n, would be lower
than the simulated values for the tax rates of the
current OASI program (column 8).

Furthermore, we may use our model to analyze one
of the most difficult problems that the OASI program
might face in the future, namely, the aging of the
population.[5] It is expected that the American
population will approach a stationary state after the
first quarter of the century.[6] Generally, the
population prospect is conditioned by two sets of
factors: (a) the demographic, and (b) the socio-econo-
mic and legal factors that condition the demographic
factors. As far as the latter set of factors is
concerned, a nation's population may become stationary
because of (a) the steadily rising cost of time, or
(b) the increasing scarcity of elements in man's
environment, or (c) both; this tendency may be partially offset by technological change which may continue
to prove resource-augmenting.

As far as the demographic factors are concerned,
they are three in number: net immigration, mortality,
and fertility. If the latter two factors do not change
over a sufficient period of time the population assumes
a "stable" age structure.

Table 7.2 below shows the ratio of the active to
the retired population under various population projections. The projections listed on the Table are
based on the following assumptions: projection W
assumes that total fertility drops immediately to the
replacement level 2.11 and remains there; projection
V assumes that total fertility falls to 1.5 by 1980
and then rises to 2.11 and remains there; projection
Z is based on the assumption that the population
becomes stationary in 1975; in all three projections
net immigration is zero; and finally, projection Z1
assumes that fertility settles at a 1.7 level after
moving below 2.0 and that net immigration continues at
400,000 per year.

The dependency ratios given on Table 7.2 are not
comparable with the Z values of Table 7.1 because of
differences in the statistical definitions of the
relevant variables; e.g., the dependency ratios in
Table 7.2 do not include the numbers of dependents of
primary retired workers. For the period 1950-1978,
about 29 percent, on the average, of the total number
of people who were receiving benefits from the OASI
program were dependents of primary retired workers;
therefore, in our calculations below we reduce all
the dependency ratios of Table 7.2 by 29 percent.

74

TABLE 7.2
Old-Age Dependency Ratios for Stationary and Stable
Populations, 1975-2050

	Number of People in Age Group 18-64 Number of People in Age Group 65+				
	1970	1985	2000	2025	2050
Projection W	5.7	5.5	5.5	3.8	3.7
Projection V	5.7	5.5	5.3	3.5	3.9
Projection Z	5.7	5.5	4.8	2.7	2.8
Projection Z1	5.6	5.5	5.1	3.2	2.9

Source: J.J. Spengler, Facing Zero Population
Growth, (Durham, N.C.: Duke University Press, 1978),
Chapter V.

        In addition to the adjustment above, we will
make the following assumptions: for the period
1985-2050, the replacement rate, γ, assumes the value
0.30, the degree of coverage variable, B, assumes
the value 0.90, and the unemployment rate is on the
average seven percent for all years.
        Then we use equation (13) of Chapter 6 to
estimate the annual payroll tax rates that are
required to support a wage-indexed pension system
which operates in an environment described by the
values of the variables mentioned above;[7]   the
estimated tax rates are shown in Table 7.3.

TABLE 7.3
Projection of Costs of the OASI Program

| Population Projection | Payroll Tax Rate As % of Average Earnings |||||
	1970	1985	2000	2025	2050
Projection W	-	9.17	9.17	13.2	13.6
Projection V	-	9.17	9.52	14.4	12.9
Projection Z	-	9.17	9.17	18.7	18.0
Projection Z1	-	9.17	9.89	15.7	17.4

Table 7.3 shows that the future costs of the
OASI program are not going to exceed current costs by
any significant proportion for the remaining part of
this century; however, substantial increases of
payroll taxes will be required after the turn of the
century provided that the economic-demographic
environment evolves according to the assumptions
stated above. Moreover, actual costs should be lower
than those shown in Table 7.3 because the OASI
program is in essence a price-indexed, not a wage-
indexed, pension system.
Finally, we should note that our estimates of
the future costs of the OASI program are very close[8]
to those derived by more formal methods.

DECOMPOSITION OF THE GROWTH RATE OF THE PAYROLL TAX

In this section we will use equations (14) and
(15) of Chapter 6 to decompose the growth rate of
the payroll tax of the U.S. OASI program for the
period 1950-1978. The two equations show how the
growth rate of the payroll tax is affected by changes
that take place, over a period of time, in the
economy or in the demographic structure of the
population. In order to obtain concrete results we
have to adopt a specific structure of the economic
and demographic environment within which the OASI
program operates. We assume a steady-state economy
in which the relevant variables assume the following
values: the growth rate of the labor force is
$n = .0611$ (the average annual compounded growth rate
for the period 1950-1978; the values of the other
variables refer to this period too); the average

growth rate of productivity is $\bar{\pi}$ = .0227; and the
average unemployment rate is .0513. Also, we set the
length of working life, m, equal to 35 years, and the
mortality rate for the retired population equal to
7.08 percent; the mortality rate is estimated as the
average of the mortality rate at age 65 (when it is
3.17 percent) and at age 80 (when it is 10.99 percent).[9]
    Using the values above we may construct Table
7.4 which shows explicitly the coefficients of the
various variables included in equations (14) and (15).
Each coefficient shows the impact on the growth rate
of the payroll tax of a unit change in the variable
shown on the top of each column.
    We may observe immediately that the influence of
the economic-demographic environment on a pay-as-you-
go pension system is, more or less, identical in both
the price-indexed and the wage-indexed versions of
this pension system. The only important difference
is that in a price-indexed system the change of the
growth rate of average productivity exercises a strong
negative influence on the cost of the program. For
example, within the specific structure we have assumed
here, we see that an one-percentage point increase in
the average productivity will subtract 0.24 percentage
points from the growth rate of the payroll tax. On
the other hand, such an influence is absent in a wage-
indexed system.
    Table 7.4 shows also the crucial importance of
the replacement rate, γ, and the degree of coverage
of the labor force by the pension system; both
variables affect equally, but in opposite direction
each, the cost of a pension system.

TABLE 7.4
The Impact of the Economic and Demographic Variables
on the Growth Rate of the Payroll Tax

	γ	B	dU/dt	dn/dt	dδ/dt	dπ/dt	dm/dt
Price-indexed System	1	-1	1.053	-30.75	-11.58	-24.47	-.03767
Wage-indexed System	1	-1	1.053	-31.62	-12.44	--	-.03767

The impact of the level of unemployment is shown to be minor in comparison to other influences; but such an effect may be important as a cost consideration because of its cyclical pattern, although in the long-run its impact might average out. According to our model, an one-percentage-point increase in the rate of unemployment will add 0.01 percentage points to the growth rate of the payroll tax.

On the other hand, an increase in the growth rate of the population by one percentage point will result, in the long-run, in a decrease of about 0.30 percentage points in the growth rate of the payroll tax. As far as the OASI program is concerned, the expected stationarity of the American population will add, at least, 0.50 (= (.0166) X (30.75)) percentage points to the growth rate of the payroll tax in the future, assuming that everything else remains constant.

Another potential source of additional costs is the rate of mortality for the people above age 65. If their life expectancy increases and this results in an one-percentage-point drop in the mortality rate, then this is going to add an extra 0.11 to 0.12 percentage points to the growth rate of the payroll tax.

Finally, the length of working life exercises a strong negative influence on the size of the payroll tax rate. An increase in working life by five years would result in the long-run in a decrease of about 0.20 percentage points in the growth rate of the payroll tax. Promoting legislation that would reduce the age of retirement would have just the opposite effect.

The analysis above permits us to derive two conclusions. First, in the short-run, the most likely sources of additional costs for the OASI program may come from increases in the replacement rate and the rate of unemployment; this effect may be offset by increases in the average productivity.

Second, in the long-run, potential sources of extra costs for the OASI program may be the decline in the growth rate of population, improvements in life expectancies at ages beyond 65, and early retirement. Whereas the first two factors are to be taken as given, the last factor may be influenced by public policy. That is, the age of retirement should be gradually increased not only in order to keep the long-run cost of the program down but also to allow for improvements in life expectancies.

For the remaining part of this section, we will use another approach to explain the variability of the growth rate of the payroll tax for the OASI program for the period 1950-1978. This analysis will serve as a test of the validity of the conclusions reached above.

The factors that accounted for most of the variability of the growth rate of the payroll tax, for the period 1950-1978, were: the replacement rate, γ; the degree of coverage of the labor force by the pension system, B; the rate of unemployment, U; the ratio of the retired to the labor force, z; and the average productivity, π. We used the method of ordinary least squares to estimate a log-linear relationship that has the payroll tax rate as the dependent variable and the variables mentioned above as the explanatory ones. The values of the dependent variable are the simulated ones shown in column (8) of Table 7.1; all the other variables are defined, and their sources are given, in Appendix B.

The estimated equation is:

$$\log (\sigma_w) = 0.181 + 1.00 \log (\gamma) - 0.905 \log B +$$
$$(4.40) \quad (24.4) \quad\quad\quad (10.3)$$

$$+ 0.048 \log U + 0.99 \log (z) - 0.0107 \log (\pi)$$
$$(2.42) \quad\quad (68.5) \quad\quad\quad (.505)$$

$$R^2 = .9994 \quad \text{and} \quad D - W = 1.780$$

The numbers in parentheses below the coefficients are the respective t-statistics. Also, the Cochrane-Orcutt test showed that autocorrelation was not a problem.

The estimated coefficients show that all variables, except average productivity, played an important role in the formation of the values of the payroll tax rates for the OASI program, for the period 1950-1978. The influence of the unemployment rate is temporary and it probably averages out in the long-run. Therefore, we may assign all the variability of the growth rate of the payroll tax to the variables γ, B, and z. In order to find the contribution of each variable to the total variability we have to transform variables γ, B, and z into growth rates.[10] The transformation is based on the fact that the average compounded growth rate of a variable X, g_x, over a period of N years is given by the formula:

$$g_x = (X_N/X_1)^{\frac{1}{N}} - 1$$

which implies that

$$\log (1 + g_x) = \frac{1}{N} \log \frac{X_N}{X_1}$$

Then, if we disregard variables U and π, and because the growth rates of γ, B, and z are very small (0.0129, 0.01307, and 0.0380 respectively, for the period 1950-1978), we may write the regression above in the following form:

$$g_\sigma = 1.00g_\gamma - 0.905g_B + 0.99g_z \qquad (1)$$

Now, if we substitute the actual growth rates of variables γ, B, and z in the equation above, we will estimate a growth rate of the payroll tax equal to 0.0387 which is almost identical with the actual growth rate of 0.0386 (because the actual payroll tax rate has increased from 3 percent in 1950 to almost 9 percent currently).

We may say that over the period 1950-1978 the growth rate of the replacement rate, γ, has increased the growth rate of the payroll tax by 33.4 percent (= (1.00 X 1.29 ÷ 3.86) X 100). Similarly, the growth rate of the ratio of the retired to the labor force, z, has raised the growth rate of the payroll tax by 97.2 percent. On the other hand, the growth rate of the degree of coverage of the population by the pension system, B, has reduced the growth rate of the payroll tax by 30.6 percent.

Finally, we should note that the coefficients of variables γ and B in equation (1) above (obtained from the regression equation) are identical to those of the respective variables in Table 7.4 which were estimated on the basis of equations (14) and (15) of Chapter 6. In addition, if we had included the U variable in equation (1), it would have had a coefficient equal to 0.048; this value is very close to the value 0.053 which is obtained (if we multiply the coefficient of the U variable from Table 7.4 by the average rate of unemployment for the period 1950-1978 (which was 0.051). The consistency of the results obtained by the two different methods provide a test for the validity of our analysis.

80

NOTES

1. For econometric models of the OASI program
see: L.H. Thompson and P.N. Van de Water, "The Short-
Run Behavior of the Social Security Trust Funds",
Public Finance Quarterly, Vol. 5, No. 3, July 1977,
pp. 351-372; and John C. Hambor, An Econometric Model
of OASDI, Studies in Income Distribution, No. 10,
Office of Research and Statistics, Social Security
Administration, U.S. Dept. of H.E.W., Washington
D.C., November 1978.
2. See J.A. Pechman, H.J. Aaron, M.K. Toussig.
Social Security: Perspectives for Reform (Washington
D.C.: Brookings Institution, 1968), pp. 204-209.
3. Ibid., Table G-2, pp. 316-317.
4. For a similar suggestion see M.D. Levy, "The
Case for Extending Social Security Coverage to
Government Employees", Journal of Risk and Insurance,
Volume XLVII, No. 1, March 1980, pp. 78-90.
5. The impact of slowing population growth on the
OASI program has been examined in a number of studies.
See: G.E. Rejda and R.J. Shepler, "The impact of
Zero Population Growth on the OASDHI Program",
Journal of Risk and Insurance, Vol. 40, September 1973,
pp. 313-325; T.D. Hogan, "The Implications of
Population Stationarity for the Social Security
System", Social Science Quarterly, Vol. 55, June 1974,
pp. 151-158; and R.L. Clark, "Increasing Income
Transfers to the Elderly implied by Zero Population
Growth", Review of Social Economy, Vol. 35, April
1977, pp. 37-54.
6. The following brief discussion is based on
J.J. Spengler, Facing Zero Population Growth (Durham,
N.C.: Duke University Press, 1978). Chapters I,
III, V.
7. We make projections for a wage-indexed pension
system because we have projected values for z, but not
for E or Λ. However, we can get an estimate of the
payroll taxes that would apply to a price-indexed
pension system by subtracting the factor $\Lambda(e^{\pi t} - 1)$
from the payroll tax rates shown in Table 7.2; this
factor is derived by subtracting equation (10) from
equation (13). To get an idea of the magnitude of
the difference between the two types of taxes we may
approximate Λ by z.
8. For a discussion of works that make estimates
of the future costs of the OASI program see: Alicia
H. Munnell, The Future of Social Security (Washington,
D.C.: Brookings Institution, 1977), Chapter 5.

9. The mortality rates mentioned are taken from the 1958 Standard Ordinary Mortality Table. See, for example, R.I. Mehr, _Life Insurance_ (Dallas, Texas: Business Publications, 1970), pp. 687-690.

10. For a description of this method see M. Morishima and M. Saito, "A Dynamic Analysis of the American Economy, 1902-1952", in _The Working of Econometric Models_ edited by M. Morishima, et al. (London: Cambridge University Press, 1972), p. 9.

Part 3

The Impact of a Pay-As-You-Go
Pension System on the Economy

8
Introduction

In Part 2 we developed a framework which may be used to analyze the influence that the economic environment exercises on a pay-as-you-go pension system. In Part 3 we will examine the system's feedback on the economy, and, in particular, the economic effects of a pay-as-you-go pension system on income and the capital stock.

The pension system influences the aggregate levels of income and the capital stock in two ways: through its effect on the ratio of aggregate saving (or investment) to aggregate income, and through its effect on the supply of labor offered for employment. Generally, a reduction in either the saving-income ratio or the fraction of the population participating in the labor force will lower income and the capital stock.

Disagreements over the effects of pay-as-you-go pension systems concern primarily the estimated reduction in the saving-income ratio.[1] Our work in Part 3 is an examination of this issue.

The first step in this type of analysis is to establish a connection between the pay-as-you-go pension system and the rest of the economy; this role is played by the social security wealth which is created by the operation of a pay-as-you-go pension system. In Chapter 9 we review Feldstein's concept of social security wealth and we argue that the way this variable is constructed overestimates the amount of wealth created by the pension system. We introduce instead a new method of measuring social security wealth.

The new variable is used in later chapters for both theoretical and empirical analyses of the impact of a pay-as-you-go pension system on capital formation and economic growth. Before doing that, we review in Chapter 10 the economic literature which deals with this issue; the basic analytical framework that has been used extensively is that of the life-cycle model

which fits in very well with Feldstein's concept of
social security wealth.
      In Chapter 11 we use a model of economic growth
which has been designed specifically to serve the
purpose of analyzing the dynamic incidence of the
national debt; this framework is more appropriate for
the public-debt-like social security wealth variable
we introduce in Chapter 9. This theoretical model
serves as the basis for a quantitative analysis, which
we undertake in Chapter 12, in order to estimate the
impact of the U.S. Old-Age and Survivors Insurance
Program on capital formation and economic growth of
the American economy.

NOTES

      1. For a theoretical analysis of the effect of
public pension systems on the supply of labor, see:
D.C. MacRae and E.C. MacRae, "Labor Supply and the
Payroll Tax" American Economic Review, Vol. 66, June
1976, pp. 408-409. Empirical evidence, for the U.S.
economy shows that social security has significantly
reduced the labor force participation rates and
working hours of older workers; see: Colin D.
Campbell and R.G. Campbell, "Conflicting Views on
the Effect of Old-Age and Survivors Insurance on
Retirement" Economic Inquiry, Vol. 14, No. 3,
September 1976, pp. 369-388; Michael J. Boskin,
"Social Security and Retirement Decisions" Economic
Inquiry Vol. 15, January 1977, pp. 1-25; Michael J.
Boskin and Michael D. Hurd, "The Effect of Social
Security on Early Retirement" Journal of Public
Economics, Vol. 10, December 1978, pp. 361-377;
Anthony J. Pellechio, The Effects of Social Security
on Retirement, National Bureau of Economic Research,
Working Paper 260, July 1978; Idem, "The Social
Security Earnings Test, Labor Supply Distortions, and
Foregone Payroll Tax Revenues, National Bureau of
Economic Research, Working Paper 272, August 1978;
and Idem, "Social Security Financing and Retirement
Behavior" American Economic Review: Papers and
Proceedings, Vol. 69, May 1979, pp. 284-287.

9
Social Security Wealth

In Part 1 we saw that an old-age pay-as-you-go
pension system is a multidimensional entity of unusual
complexity. After careful inspection, however, two
important characteristics of this system may be
discerned. First, for purposes of short-run analysis
the best way to view a pay-as-you-go pension system
is that of a tax-transfer mechanism that redistributes
income between successive generations. This approach
was utilized in Chapter 6 to analyze the operation of
the system in the short-run. Within a framework of
long-run analysis, however, the tax of the tax-transfer
mechanism is transformed into a contribution to a
pension plan providing retirement and survivorship
benefits. This second characteristic of a pay-as-you-
go pension system implies an additional asset to the
other assets of covered workers and their families.
Each such household may enjoy the expectation of price-
indexed retirement income to be provided by the
government as a matter of right at the end of their
working years. This "social security wealth" is an
important, though often neglected, part of their
total assets.

The concept of the social security wealth was
introduced in the economic literature for the purpose
of establishing an analytical connection between the
pay-as-you-go pension system and the rest of the
economy. The wealth effect of a pay-as-you-go pension
system is basic to any analysis of its effects on the
supply of labor, private saving and investment, and
the economy's rate of growth. However, the conclusions of these analyses may be sensitive to the way
that the social security wealth concept is conceived
of or estimated. Before taking a position on this
issue we shall review the existing literature.

FELDSTEIN'S CONCEPT OF SOCIAL SECURITY WEALTH

Feldstein was the first to introduce formally the concept of the social security wealth.[1] He conceived of this as a component of household wealth or, more accurately, of household fungible wealth.[2] He developed two measures of the social security wealth. The first, the Gross Social Security Wealth (GSSW), is the actuarial present value of the social security benefits to which an individual or family will become entitled at age 65. The second, the Net Social Security Wealth (NSSW), is the difference between the actuarial present value of all future retirement benefits for an individual and the actuarial present value of all future payroll taxes to be paid by this individual.

The basic logic of the calculations used to evaluate GSSW and NSSW can be explained briefly. It is assumed that a worker, who is of age x presently, will be entitled to an annual social security benefit in the amount b when he retires at age 65. The calculation assumes that b is 0.41 times per capita disposable income in year t + 65 - x when the individual retires, Y_{t+65-x}. This future value of disposable income is estimated by assuming that disposable per capita income grows at the rate g annually. In addition, it is assumed that pensions are wage-indexed, that the retirement period is from age 65 to age 100, and that S_{ij} denotes the probability that a man age i survives to at least age j. Then, the social security annuity at age 65, for the worker, will have a value of:

$$\int_{65}^{100} S_{65,t} \cdot (0.41) \cdot Y_o \cdot e^{((65-x) + (t-65))g} \cdot dt \tag{1}$$

where Y_o is per capita disposable income in the present period. The gross social security wealth for the worker, at the present time, is the discounted value of (1). To calculate the NSSW variable, it is necessary to estimate the present discounted value of the payroll taxes that will be paid by the worker and to subtract this value from the gross social security wealth.

Certain observations should be made concerning Feldstein's concepts of social security wealth.

First, Feldstein's analysis is an extension or a modification of the modern theories of consumption.

According to these theories it is an individual's
wealth, that is, the present value of his lifetime
income, that determines how much consumption he can
enjoy during his lifetime. Feldstein creates the
social security wealth as a component of total household wealth in order to establish an analytical
relationship between public pension systems and
consumption.

Second, it is not clear from Feldstein's analysis
which of the two social security wealth concepts is
the most appropriate. We would argue that the concept
of Gross Social Security Wealth is based on the idea
that the payroll tax is a substitute for private
savings; that is, people conceive of the payroll tax
as a type of compulsory savings. On the other hand,
it seems that the concept of Net Social Security
Wealth is based on the idea that the payroll tax is
indeed a tax, and, therefore, this measure of social
security wealth shows an individual's net potential
loss should the public pension program suddenly be
eliminated (or gain from its continuing existence).

From what was said earlier (see discussion in
Chapter 5) it seems that the GSSW is the appropriate
concept of wealth associated with a public pension
system. The NSSW concept is better suited for budget-
incidence analyses of the public pension program which
analyses try to disentangle the distributional equity
of the program. Indeed, this concept has been used
for this type of incidence analyses.[3]

Third, it must be made clear that the Gross
Social Security Wealth is not the same concept as the
more commonly used concept of "pension wealth". The
latter, associated with actuarial estimates in private
pension plans, refers to the present value of
expected benefits already earned, whereas the GSSW
refers to the present value of expected benefits.
This concept has been used by Feldstein to examine how
the distribution of household wealth is modified when
the GSSW is included in household wealth. He finds
that the distribution of wealth is greatly modified
and a great deal of the existing inequality is reduced
when the GSSW is included among the household assets.[4]

We generally agree with the usage of the concept
of gross social security wealth to modify the distribution of wealth, although we disagree with the way
this wealth concept is calculated. We also agree on
the issue that the payroll taxes should be excluded
from the analysis in this context, although, as we
mentioned above, the NSSW concept may be the
appropriate one for budget-incidence analyses of the
public pension system. But in a case of absolute-
incidence analysis of the benefits of a public pension

system the taxes have no role to play.

Our objection to the way that the GSSW is calculated is that this method assigns to each worker an amount of wealth that has not been earned. For example, if we accept Feldstein's analyses, we will have to endow every worker who just enters the labor force with a large amount of wealth that he will receive when he retires; that is, this wealth is assigned automatically to the new worker although the expected pension benefits have not been earned yet. It seems to us that the proper approach would be to build up a worker's social security wealth by adding the annual increments of wealth that the worker "earns" with his contributions to the pension system. This approach will be examined next.

A NEW CONCEPT OF SOCIAL SECURITY WEALTH

We are going to consider social security wealth as a variant of national debt. This is not a new way of looking at the operation of a pay-as-you-go pension system,[5] but it is new in our context.

The basic point of this analysis is to view the total amount of annual payroll taxes as being used to finance an issue of new national debt. The revenue is used to finance the pensions of the current pensioners, but this transaction creates a liability which is assumed by the government. This liability is the total amount of claims of the people who "hold" this year's, newly issued, debt. The maturity period of this debt is equal to the number of remaining years in one's working life. Moreover, it is compulsory for members of the labor force to buy specific amounts of debt every year, and in addition, such an asset is not exchangeable.[6]

If we call this asset a "pension bond", then as we will show presently, the rate of return on this bond is the sum of the growth rates of the taxable base and the tax rate which applies on that base. The taxable base, which is aggregate earnings, grows by an amount equal to the growth rate of the labor force, n, plus the growth rate of real average earnings (or average productivity), π. As far as the tax rate, σ_w, is concerned, we saw in Chapter 6 that the growth rate of the payroll tax changes with changes in various economic and demographic variables.

To illustrate the point made in the previous paragraph, consider an economy in which employment is growing at rate n, and real wages at rate π. Assume, also, to simplify the illustration, that people work

for one year, retire for one year and then die.
Assume wages are w_o in the year the pension system
starts up, that workers pay a tax of σ_w percent
of their wages, and that the political-economic-
demographic situation is such that the tax rate grows
at an annual rate t percent. In the first year the
tax revenues will be $\sigma_w \cdot w_o$. In the second year,
the tax revenue will be $\sigma_w \cdot w_o \cdot e^{n+\pi+t}$, due to
increases in the tax base and the tax rate;
therefore, the second generation of retirees will
receive a rate of return on its contributions of 100 ·
$(n+\pi+t)$ percent. If the tax rate is kept constant,
then the rate of return on all subsequent generations
will be equal to $n+\pi$, which is what we wanted to
prove. As far as the constancy of the tax rate is
concerned, we may recall, from Chapter 6 that this
rate will, more or less, stabilize when the pension
system reaches its maturity stage, and the population
becomes stationary (for more detailed information
refer to equations (14) and (15) of Chapter 6).

For our purposes, an important observation is in
order: as the pay-as-you-go pension system reaches its
stage of maturity, people will gradually come to
realize that their "contributions" to the pension
system will grow at a rate which is equal to the
growth rate of the economy. Moreover, it is more
reasonable to assume that the average worker perceives
of his social security wealth as the compounded value
of his annual "contributions", than to assume that he
perceives of his social security wealth as the present
discounted value of his expected pension benefits to
which he will be entitled after he retires.

If this logic is accepted, then we may estimate
the social security wealth of the "average" worker as
the total value of the "pension bonds" which he has
acquired during his working life. If we call this
wealth F_i, it is:

$$F_i = \int_0^m (\sigma_w \cdot w_o \cdot e^{(b+\pi) t}) \cdot e^{(n+\pi)(m-t)} \cdot dt$$

or

$$F_i = \frac{\sigma_w \cdot w_o}{b - n} \cdot e^{(n+\pi) m} (e^{(b-n) m} - 1) \qquad (2)$$

where m is the length of working life, b is the rate
of inflation, and w_o is the annual wage of year zero.

Expression (2) is an estimate of the social security
wealth for the "average" worker who has contributed,
for m years, σ_w percent of his annual earnings to the
pension system, provided that annual contributions
compound annually at $\pi+n$. We note that the "average"
worker's earnings grow at $b+\pi$ annually, whereas real
aggregate earnings per capita grow at $\pi+n$ annually.

The amount of social security wealth estimated [7]
above refers to the last year of one's working life.
For any specific year, during one's working life, the
amount of social security wealth is less than the
amount shown in (2). As one accumulates "pension
bonds" his social security wealth increases, reaching
its maximum value at the final year of working life.

At any year t, the social security wealth of a
worker depends on his age and the number of years he
has contributed to the system. In the aggregate, the
total amount of "pension bonds" issued in a specific
year t could be found by summing up the pension bonds
obtained by workers in this pecific year. This
magnitude would represent the annual change in the
national debt, that is, the deficit for year t. The
expression "national debt" here refers to the
obligation of the government to redeem all "pension
bonds" when they are presented in the future (when
each worker retires).

In order to calculate the social security wealth
for any year t, we will have to use the demographic
model which is developed in Appendix A. According to
this model, people enter the labor force at the age of
16 and retire at the beginning of the year when they
attain age 65. Each worker pays σ_w percent of his
annual wage, w_t, in payroll taxes. This amount of
money buys him a "pension bond" with a rate of return
$n+\pi$ over the period of his working life, which is 48
years. Every year B_t percent of the labor force is
covered by the pension system, and the unemployment
rates is U_t. The growth rate of the labor force is
n, and the average productivity is π.

Every year the labor force consists of age
cohorts from age 16 to age 64. Each age cohort is
equal to f_{16+k} percent of the labor force, L_t, where
f_{16+k} is given by the expression:

$$f_{16+k} = \frac{n \cdot e^{n(48-k)}}{e^{48n} - 1} \quad , \; \forall \; k = 0, \; 1,2,\ldots 48.$$

At year t, workers in the age cohort 16 expect their annual contribution to accumulate for 48 years at the compound interest $n+\pi$; workers in the age cohor 17 expect their annual contribution to compound for 47 years, etc.

More analytically, the value of "pension bonds", for year t, for each age cohort is:

Cohort of Age 16: $(\sigma_w \cdot w_t) \cdot f_{16} \cdot L_t \cdot e^{48(n+\pi)} \cdot$

$\cdot B_t \cdot (1 - U_t)$

Cohort of Age 17: $(\sigma_w \cdot w_t) \cdot f_{17} \cdot L_t \cdot e^{47(n+\pi)} \cdot$

$\cdot B_t \cdot (1 - U_t)$

$\vdots$ $\vdots$

Cohort of Age 64: $(\sigma_w \cdot w_t) \cdot f_{64} \cdot L_t \cdot e^{0(n+\pi)} \cdot$

$\cdot B_t \cdot (1 - U_t)$

Now if we substitute f_{16+k} for the appropriate year and sum up over all age cohorts we will derive the total pension bonds for year t, or the social security wealth, F, "earned" by the labor force in year t. We emphasize the expression "earned pension bonds", because this is one of the basic differences between our approach and Feldstein's.

It is:

$$F = \sigma_w \cdot w_t \cdot B_t \cdot (1-U_t) \cdot L_t \cdot \frac{n}{e^{48n}-1} \, (e^{48n} \cdot e^{48(n+\pi)} +$$

$$+ \ldots + 1 \cdot 1 \,)$$

$$= \sigma_w \cdot w_t \cdot B_t \cdot (1-U_t) \cdot L_t \cdot \frac{n}{e^{48n}-1} \cdot \int_o^{48} e^{nt} \cdot e^{(n+\pi)} dt$$

or

$$F = \sigma_w \cdot w_t \cdot B_t \cdot (1-U_t) \cdot L_t \cdot \frac{n}{2n+\pi} \, \frac{1}{e^{48n}-1} \cdot (e^{48(2n+\pi)}-1)$$

$$(3)$$

Now, if we continue assuming that it may make
little difference whether the national debt is
evidenced by Treasury bills, notes, or bonds or
whether it consists of the promisory liabilities for
social security benefits accrued by the government,
then we may consider expression (3) as the annual
deficit incurred by the government in the public
pensions sector. Integrating over a period of time
we may derive the social security wealth that has
been accumulated by the labor force during this
period of time.

Using operational data from the U.S. OASI system
we may calculate annual values for expression (3).
Our estimates cover the period 1950-1978. During
this period the average compound growth rate of the
labor force was 1.66 percent annually and the average
rate of growth in productivity for this period was
2.27 percent; hence, the growth rate of real aggregate
earnings over the period 1950-1978 is assumed to be
3.93 percent annually. The payroll tax rates, σ_w,
used in our estimates are the statutory ones.
These taxes are imposed every year on wages up to the
"maximum taxable earnings base"; hence, w_t in
expression (3) refers to average taxable earnings
per covered worker. More accurate description of all
variables in (3), as well as their sources, are given
in Appendix B. Finally, we should note that the
number 48 in expression (3) stands for the length
of working life, m, but we have also estimated F by
using m = 30 years and m = 35 years. The estimated
annual values of F, found from (3), are expressed in
current dollars. We transformed them into constant
dollar by using the deflator for personal consumption
expenditures (1972 = 100).

Our estimates are presented in Table 9.1. This
table shows the annual increments in social security
wealth, expressed in constant 1972 dollars, for the
total labor force. The total amount of accumulated
social security wealth that was created by the OASI
program during the period 1950-1978 is 1.286 trillion
dollars when m = 30 years, 1.394 trillion dollars when
m = 35 years, and 1.864 trillion dollars when m = 48
years. Feldstein's latest estimate is that in 1977
the accumulated social security wealth was 4.082
trillion in constant 1972 dollars.[8]

TABLE 9.1
Estimated Annual Social Security Wealth of the OASI
Program (millions of 1972 Dollars)

Year	When m = 30 years	When m = 35 years	When m = 48 years
1950	8,186.2	8,869.2	11,860.9
1951	10,795.7	11,696.4	15,641.6
1952	12,255.6	13,278.1	17,756.9
1953	11,988.4	12,988.7	17,369.9
1954	14,498.5	16,031.1	21,438.4
1955	18,187.8	19,705.3	26,352.1
1956	19,362.9	20,978.5	28,054.6
1957	19,163.1	20,762.0	27,765.1
1958	18,134.3	19,647.3	26,274.4
1959	23,194.6	25,129.9	33,606.3
1960	28,352.4	30,717.9	41,079.3
1961	27,893.9	30,221.2	40,415.0
1962	30,644.1	33,200.9	44,399.8
1963	36,421.3	39,460.0	52,770.2
1964	38,022.5	41,194.9	55,090.2
1965	40,024.9	43,364.3	57,991.4
1966	49,744.6	53,895.0	72,074.1
1967	50,899.8	55,146.6	73,747.9
1968	52,462.5	56,839.7	76,012.0
1969	59,975.4	64,979,4	86,897.4
1970	56,601.8	61,324.3	82,009.4
1971	61,258.2	66,369.3	88,756.1
1972	67,964.2	73,634.7	98,472.2
1973	80,962.5	87,717.6	117,305.0
1974	81,665.7	88,479.4	118,324.0
1975	77,597.1	84,071.3	112,429.0
1976	85,534.8	92,671.3	123,930.0
1977	98,039.8	106,220.0	142,048.0
1978	106,625.0	115,521.0	154,487.0
TOTAL	1,286,742.0	1,394,041.9	1,864,349.0
Average	44,370.4	48,070.4	64,287.9

Moreover, as we may see from Table 9.1, the annual deficit of the government's debt for pensions changes over the business cycle and, also, changes because of changes in the demographic or structural variables that affect it. In order to see this type of influence more clearly, we will take the logarithmic derivative of expression (3) with respect to time. After simplifying we obtain:

$$\dot{F} = \dot{\sigma}_w + \dot{B}_t + \dot{w}_t + \dot{L}_t - \frac{1}{1-U}\frac{dU}{dt} +$$

$$+ \left(\frac{1}{n} + \frac{2m \cdot e^{m(2n+\pi)}}{e^{m(2n+\pi)} - 1} - \frac{2}{2n+\pi} - \frac{m}{e^{nm}}\frac{e^{nm}}{-1}\right)\frac{dn}{dt} +$$

$$+ \left(\frac{m \cdot e^{m(2n+\pi)}}{e^{m(2n+\pi)} - 1} - \frac{1}{2n+\pi}\right)\frac{d\pi}{dt}$$

(4)

This equation shows that the growth rate of the annual deficit (annual social security wealth), $\dot{F}$, is the sum of the growth rates of the payroll tax rate, $\dot{\sigma}_w$, pension coverage of the labor force, $\dot{B}_t$, real average taxable earnings, $\dot{w}_t$, and labor force, $\dot{L}_t$. In addition, the growth rate of the deficit increases with increases in the growth rate of productivity, and decreases with increases in unemployment.

If we want to obtain specific values for the coefficients in equation (4), we may use the following values: $n = .0166$, $\pi = .0227$, $m = 35$, and $\bar{U} = .0513$. Those values were calculated from the actual data of the OASI program for the period 1950-1978. Then, we may rewrite (4) as follows:

$$\dot{F} = \dot{\sigma}_w + \dot{B}_t + \dot{w}_t + \dot{L}_t - (1.054)\frac{dU}{dt} + (43.41)\frac{dn}{dt}$$

$$+ (22.89)\frac{d\pi}{dt}$$

(5)

We may observe from (5) that the annual deficit will stabilize only when the pension system matures completely (then $\dot{\sigma}_w = 0$, and $\dot{B}_t = 0$) and the population becomes stationary and/or stable (then $\dot{L}_t = 0$). In such a case only cyclical disturbances will affect the magnitude of the annual deficit of the government's pension debt; such cyclical disturbances arise in our model from changes in productivity

π, and unemployment, U.

Moreover, equation (5) shows that the growth rate of social security wealth, $\dot{F}$, increases directly with increases in the growth rates of σ_w, B, w, and L. In addition, equation (5) shows that an one-percentage-point increase in the rate of unemployment will subtract 0.01 percentage points from the growth rate of F, whereas an one-percentage-point increase in productivity, will add 0.23 percentage points to the growth rate of social security wealth.

NOTES

1. Martin Feldstein, "Social Security, Induced Retirement, and Aggregate Capital Accumulation", Journal of Political Economy, Vol. 82, No. 5, Sept./ October 1974, pp. 505-927.

2. The components of household wealth are: (1) Financial investment assets, (2) business net worth, (3) real estate, (4) automobiles, (5) consumer durables other than automobiles, (6) cash value life insurance, (7) present value of private pension benefits. Feldstein called household fungible wealth the total value of the first four items minus all debts.

3. See Martin Feldstein and Anthony Pellechio, Social Security Wealth: The Impact of Alternative Inflation Adjustments, National Bureau of Economic Research, Working Paper 212, November 1977; and also J.E. Pesando and S.A. Rea, Public and Private Pensions in Canada: An Economic Analysis, Ontario Economic Council Research Studies No. 9, (Toronto: University of Toronto Press, 1977), Chapter 7.

4. Martin Feldstein, "Social Security and the Distribution of Wealth", Journal of the American Statistical Association, Vol. 71, No. 356, December 1976, pp. 800-807.

5. See Browning, E.K., "Social Insurance and Inter-generational Transfers", Journal of Law and Economics Vol. 16, October 1973, pp. 215-237, and Robert Barro, "Are Government Bonds Net Wealth?", Journal of Political Economy, Vol. 82, Nov./Dec. 1974, pp. 1095-1117. See, also, the exchange between Barro and Feldstein, Buchanan in the Journal of Political Economy, Nol. 84, No. 2, April 1976, pp. 331-349.

6. For a discussion of the issues of maturity, marketability, and compulsion as they relate to issues of national debt see: Richard Musgrave, The

98

Theory of Public Finance (New York: McGraw-Hill Book
Co., 1959), pp. 583-587.
    7. In order to show more explicitly the differ-
ences between Feldstein's method and ours, we may
estimate the amount of social security wealth, at age
65, for an average worker who pays σ_w percent of his
annual disposable income in payroll taxes. If
disposable income per capital, Y, grows at the rate
g = π + n, then the amount of social security wealth
according to our method will be:

$$\sigma_w \cdot Y_0 \cdot m \cdot e^{mg}$$

where m is length of working life. By using equation
(1), we may estimate social security wealth, at age
65, according to Feldstein's approach. It is:

$$(0.41) \cdot Y_0 \cdot \frac{1}{g} \cdot e^{-65g} \cdot e^{(100 - 65)g}$$

    8. See Martin Feldstein, _Government Deficits and
Aggregate Demand_, National Bureau of Economic Research,
Working Paper No. 435, January 1980, p. 36.

10
The Impact of a Pay-As-You-Go Pension System on the Economy: Review of the Literature

As we saw in the previous chapter the operation of a pay-as-you-go pension system creates a new and important form of household wealth. By adding an entirely new dimension to individual economic welfare, social security has altered behavior in a number of important ways. People retire earlier than they otherwise would. Earlier retirement may strengthen incentives to save for a longer retirement period. On the other hand, the very operation of a pay-as-you-go pension system creates promises of pension benefits that might lessen the need to save for retirement and hence may replace household saving that otherwise would have occurred.

The most important economic effect of a pay-as-you-go pension system is its impact on capital formation and economic growth. An economic analysis of this topic involves the discussion of three separate issues.

First, it must be decided whether and by how much the present rate of capital formation is inadequate. Methodologically, this would require an analysis of capital markets. Beginning with the supply side, a constraint in the availability of savings and investible funds should be signaled by a high and rising real rate of interest. On the demand side of a capital market the willingness to invest is largely dependent on the after tax rates of return.[1] Moreover, from the point of view of the theory of economic growth, a level of capital which is lower than the "optimal" would be indicated by a real rate of interest, r, which would be greater than the growth rate of output, g, for the economy. For most industrial economies it is: $r > g$, but, as we will argue in the last section of this chapter, this does not imply inefficiency.

Second, an attempt must be made to identify the limiting factors which have kept capital from being larger.[2] The second and third sections of this chapter

shall be devoted to a critical review of theoretical
and empirical works which try to determine the impact
of a pay-as-you-go pension system on the rate of
capital formation.

The third issue involves a discussion of the
policy implications of the problems detected in the
first two steps, and an evaluation of the alternative
techniques that may be used to deal with these
problems. Those who advocate that the pay-as-you-go
pension system has reduced capital have proposed full
funding of the public pension system because they
see this as a way of increasing capital formation.
The merit of this argument will be examined in the
fourth section of this chapter.

From a methodological point of view, the impact
of a pay-as-you-go pension system on capital
formation may be examined by using a differential-
incidence approach; that is, whatever the gross
effects of a public pension system on saving may be,
it is the net, or incremental, effects that really
matter for policy purposes. In other words, if the
public pension system had never been established, the
most likely alternative development would have been
that private pension plans would have expanded more
rapidly than they have. If these plans are fully
funded and vested, they basically substitute business
saving for household saving. The composition, but not
the total amount, of private saving would be changed
as a result. If a pay-as-you-go pension system
discourages personal saving, for any of the reasons
that will be discussed below, the net impact of its
substitution for private pension plans would be a
reduction in national saving. This would cause an
efficiency loss which should be avoided. This
methodological point is discussed briefly in the
following section.

THE EXCESS BURDEN OF A PAY-AS-YOU-GO PENSION SYSTEM

Martin Feldstein's argument about the potential
adverse effect of a pay-as-you-go pension system on
the rate of capital formation and economic growth is
based on a differential incidence analysis[3] where
the pay-as-you-go pension system is set against a
private pension system. Eventually, the net effect
of this comparison is what matters for policy
purposes; that is, it must be proved that private
pensions do not reduce aggregate savings while a pay-
as-you-go pension system does.

As far as the theoretical issues are concerned, a private pension system will have no effect on aggregate savings if three conditions are satisfied:[4] (1) employees regard the annual increase in the present actuarial value of their future pensions as an equivalent increase in their wealth, (2) employees reduce their direct personal savings to keep the sum of this direct saving and the increased value of future pension benefits unchanged, and (3) full funding of pension plans. Feldstein mentions five cases where the first two conditions may not be satisfied;[5] but the overall effect on aggregate saving is ambiguous.

Moreover, the third assumption is also not satisfied in practice, but economic analysis suggests that in this case the response of companies and their shareholders will compensate for the unfunded pension liabilities. Indeed, such liabilities although not explicitly stated in financial statements, will eventually make themselves felt in one of two ways: (1) reduced stock prices (and therefore reduction in capital gains) due to the "awareness effect" in stock markets,[6] or (2) increased retained earnings or dividends. It may be assumed that decreased capital gains and increased dividends will both result in higher savings. Moreover, there is some evidence that reduced retained earnings (due to higher dividends) will provoke more saving.[7] However, the validity of these conclusions is questionable.

We may conclude that the theoretical questions associated with the effect of private pensions on aggregate saving do not as yet have a satisfactory agreed upon answer. Unfortunately, the limited empirical evidence that is available on this issue consists of contradictory results.[8] This raises the possibility that any estimated reduction in aggregate saving may be assigned to both the pay-as-you-go pension system and the private pension system (in both cases because of unfunded liabilities). Generally, it may be said that the private pension system increases total saving but by less than the full actuarial value of the promised pension benefits. Hence, substitution of an unfunded pay-as-you-go pension system for a substantially (but not fully) funded system of private pensions should reduce saving by less than the negative impact the public pension system itself has on personal saving. However, all theories that have been developed to analyze and measure this effect deal basically with the gross effect of public pensions on saving. We turn to these theories now.

THE EFFECT OF PUBLIC PENSIONS ON SAVING

Various theoretical frameworks have been developed to analyze the effect of a pay-as-you-go pension system on personal savings.

The most often used theoretical model so far has been the "extended life-cycle model", which is an extension of the life-cycle model of consumption; the extension was made by Feldstein.[9]

Feldstein's theoretical model has been extended by the works of Hemming (continuous time life-cycle model), Hu (allows for an explicit retirement decision as opposed to the traditional view of fixed retirement duration) and Kotlikoff (who introduced explicitly the "yield effect").[10]

In the extended life-cycle model households save during their working years to finance consumption during retirement, and in the simplest version of the model the working and retirement phases are of fixed duration. In such a world a pay-as-you-go pension system provides a substitute to private saving for achieving the same goal. In principle, this substitution should be an exact one for any actuarially fair social security system (actuarially fair means that the present value of payroll taxes equals the present value of pensions). In such a case payroll tax contributions would not come at the expense of consumption but would reduce savings on a dollar-for-dollar basis; this is the "replacement effect". In addition, the "yield effect" will be generated by systems with rates of return above or below the market rate of interest; savings would be reduced or increased respectively. Moreover, if we relax the assumption of fixed periods of work and retirement, then the "retirement effect" might arise because social security induces early retirement; this effect is expected to increase savings.

Before we proceed to examine alternative theories we may make certain comments concerning the three effects that are derived from the extended life-cycle model.

As far as the retirement effect is concerned, it is generally agreed that it increases savings, and that as the social security system matures this effect should decline in importance.

As far as the yield effect is concerned, it is logical to assume that it would be sustantial in the early years of the operation of a social security system. But this effect, in this case, would affect

savings only if people had perfect knowledge, an
important assumption of all life-cycle models. The
only econometric evidence for this effect, based on
American experience, shows that this effect is not
statistically significant, which confirms the
suspicions that households might not have perfect
foresight.[11]   Moreover, when the pension system
matures the rate of return on payroll tax contributions will stabilize at a rate equal to the growth
rate of the economy. Then, we might expect households to realize this fact and behave accordingly,
that is, they might even increase their savings if
the rate of return on contributions is less than the
market rate of interest.

As far as the replacement effect is concerned,
its importance is partially reduced because of
illiquidities associated with social security
benefits; that is, a current worker who pays payroll
taxes currently cannot borrow against future income
(from pensions) because of capital market imperfections (perfect capital markets is another implicit
assumption of life cycle models). To the degree that
there are a large number of liquidity-constrained
households (that is, those households would not have
saved at all in the absence of the social security
system or in the early years of their working lives),
we cannot assume that those households have compensa-
ted for their benefits in the future by reducing other
savings or provisions for retirement.

Feldstein's analysis has been challenged by Barro,
who views social security as a government-imposed
system of intergenerational transfers that is
analogous to public debt issues.[12]   Barro's model
differs from Feldstein's in that it introduces
bequests - i.e., private intergenerational transfers.
His analysis indicates that the individuals in his
model could offset the effects of the introduction
of social security by changing their bequests. This
offsetting action is completely effective when all
the individuals have the same tastes, productivity,
endowments, social security coverage, and tax
liabilities, and where retirement age is unaffected
by the introduction of social security. As far as
the "bequest effect" is concerned, it is usually
assumed to be zero in most econometric studies of the
impact of a pay-as-you-go pension system on savings
and investment. However, recent works have shown
that the magnitude of this effect may be susbstantial.[13]
On the other hand, it must be admitted that it is
difficult to say exactly how people might relate their
bequest plans to the way the social security system
operates.

In addition to the life-cycle models, some other theories have been developed to explain the influence of a pay-as-you-go pension system on savings and investment.

First, there are the behavioral models of Cagan and Katona.[14] They suggest that social security may actually increase saving, either because the presence of the system makes people aware of their future retirement needs (Cagan), or because the very existence of private or public pension systems converts retirement support from an unattainable little-thought-of goal to a reasonably attainable one (Katona). It seems that those theories might have some importance during the early years of a pension system, but they are unlikely to apply to a mature pension system.

Another more sophisticated theory of an inter-generational social contract model views an unfunded social security system as a rational response to market imperfections that keep the rate of return on investment in human capital higher than rates of return on physical capital.[15] The implicit social contract, in this model, is a stronger parental commitment to education of children, and this invest-ment in human capital would then yield a higher retire-ment annuity to the parents when they retire. The higher annuity would be due to higher current earnings (higher growth of real wages) of the children who would have benefitted from the higher investment in education.

As a description of what ought to be this model raises important questions but provides few answers. As a description of how people really behave this model assumes a level of rationality and knowledge that few possess.

EMPIRICAL EVIDENCE

Admittedly, a potential negative impact of the pay-as-you-go pension system on the rate of capital formation and therefore the level of economic growth must be an issue of great public concern. As we saw in the previous section, theory cannot answer this question in a definitive manner. It is only logical then that economists have turned to empirical estimates of any potential negative impact of the

social security on saving and investment. As Table
10.1 shows,[16]   during the last six years more
than a dozen studies have been undertaken to examine
this issue. With the exception of four studies which
use a cross-section of various industrialized
countries, all of the other studies refer to the
impact of the OASI program on the American economy.
    Feldstein, who did the pioneering work on this
subject,[17]   has been the leading voice of the
group of economists who attribute a significant
decline in national saving to the social security
program as it has developed during the postwar period.
Feldstein's last word on the subject[18]   is that,
at 1972 national income levels, social security
reduced private saving by $ 44 billion, or 59 percent
of actual saving in that year. Concerning this
result, it has been argued that "No evidence is
sufficient to establish an implausible result unless
the unreliability of the evidence would be more
remarkable than the result which it endeavors to
establish." [19]
    From a technical point of view, most of the
studies cited in Table 10.1 use as the basic
estimated equation a consumption (or savings) function;
but the studies differ in the way they specify these
functions. There is a great variety of variables
used, methods of estimating those variables,
definitions, etc.[20]
    In six of the studies[20]   listed in Table
10.1, Feldstein has used as his basic regression
equation a consumption function derived from his
extended life-cycle theory. He tests for the
significance of the social security wealth variable
(see Chapter 9). Two of the six studies (1977, 1979b)
use information derived from a cross-section of 12-15
countries; three studies (1974, 1979a, 1980) use
macro-data from the U.S. OASI program; and the 1979
study (with A. Pellechio) uses a micro-data set
collected by the Federal Reserve Board in 1963.
Although the earlier studies do not give statistically significant results (however, Feldstein interprets
the results as if they were significant), the 1979(a)
study, which is based on revised estimates of
national income and its components (made by the
Department of Commerce), yields the statistically
significant result mentioned above.
    Supportive of Feldstein's results are the
studies made by Kotlikoff and Munnell.[21]
Munnell in her 1974 study tests for the impact of
social security on both total private savings and
retirement savings; the latter is defined as house-

TABLE 10.1
Empirical Studies of the Effects of Social Security on Saving

Authors	Data Set	Social Security Variables	Findings
1. Barro (1978)	Macro time series 1929-40, 1947-74	Gross social security wealth; benefits per recipient times proportion of labor force covered	No effects
2. Barro and Mac-Donald (1979)	16 industrialized countries, 1951-60	Benefits per recipient	Inconclusive
3. Darby (1979)	Macro time series, 1929-40, 1947-74	Gross and net social security wealth; benefits per recipient times proportion of labor force covered times population; OASI taxes	Negative or zero
4. Feldstein (1974)	Macro time series, 1929-40, 1947-71	Gross and net social security wealth	Significant negative effect
5. Feldstein (1977)	15 industrialized countries, 1954-60	Benefits per recipient; eligibility ratio; age of system	Support for extended life cycle model; negative saving effects
6. Feldstein (1979a)	Macro time series, 1929-40, 1947-74	Gross social security wealth	Significant negative effect

Study	Sample/Data	Variables	Results
7. Feldstein (1979b)	12 industrial countries, 1969-75	Benefits per recipient; benefit replacement ratio; age of system	Support for extended life cycle model; negative saving effects
8. Feldstein (1980)	Macro time series 1930-40, 1947-77	Social security wealth	Significant negative effect
9. Feldstein and Pellechio (1979)	Federal Reserve Board, Survey of Financial Characteristics of Consumers, 1963; Households headed by Insured males, 55-64	Net social security wealth	Significant negative effect
10. Kopits and Gotur (1980)	14 industrial countries; 1969-71	Benefits per recipient; social security taxes; age of system	Positive saving effects
	40 developing countries, 1969-71		No effects
11. Kotlikoff (1979a)	Theoretical model of equilibrium steady state capital stock	Social security tax and benefit rates	Potentially large negative effects on capital stock

108

"Table 10.1 (cont'd)"
Empirical Studies of the Effects of Social Security on Saving

Authors	Data Set	Social Security Variables	Findings
12. Kotlikoff(1979b)	1966 National Longitudinal Survey of men aged 45-59	Lifetime social security wealth increments	No effects
		Accumulated value of employee and employer taxes paid per household	Negative effect
13. Munnell(1974)	Macro time series, 1900-71	Social security wealth	Support for extended life cycle model
		Employee and employer taxes	Negative saving effects

Source: George F. Break, "The Economic Effects of Social Security's OASI Program" (University of California, Berkeley, March 1980), mimeo, pp. 32-33.

hold assets that are accumulated primarily to provide
support and security during old age (this group of
assets consists of the net increase in assets of life
insurance companies, business pension plans, and
government insurance and pension plans). The impact
of social security on private savings (total and
retirement) is measured in two different ways: by a
social security wealth variable (like Feldstein's) and
by employer-employee payroll taxes viewed as a proxy
for expected benefits. In the estimated regressions
the wealth variable outperforms the tax proxy and the
social security effects show up more significantly in
the retirement, than in the total, savings equations.
The opposing wealth and retirement effects give a net
effect on retirement savings in 1969 equal to -2.9
billion in 1958 dollars or some 8 percent of total
savings in that year. This estimate, of course,
assumes that social security has no impact on nonreti-
rement saving, which was the more important component
during most of the years studied. In addition, Munnell
notes that the negative net impact on retirement saving
is likely to increase in the future because the
decline in labor force participation rates of older
workers is slowing at the same time that social
security benefit increases are accelerating.

Kotlikoff's 1979(a) study is based on a theoretical model which uses both partial and general equilibrium analyses to isolate the potential effects of
social security's wealth and retirement effects on an
economy's steady-state capital stock. Given certain
plausible values of the various parameters, the model
suggests a 20 percent reduction in the capital stock
in the case of general equilibrium analysis, whereas
the steady-state capital stock is reduced substantially
more when partial equilibrium analysis is used.

Kotlikoff's second study (1979b) uses a sample of
men aged 45-59 selected from the National Longitudinal
Survey taken by the Bureau of the Census in 1966 and
later years. He uses separate variables to account
for the replacement effect (the variable used has
certain similarities to the social security wealth
variable that we proposed in Chapter 9), the yield
effect (the variable used is similar to Feldstein's
net social security wealth variable), and the retirement effect. It turns out that the yield effect is
not statistically significant, whereas the other two
effects are. The coefficient for the replacement
effect is -0.67; this negative effect is only partially
offset by a very small retirement effect. However, as
the author of the study admits, a negative replacement
effect does not confirm the analytical validity of the
life-cycle model because even a Keynesian savings

function would show reduced savings due to reduced disposable income (because of the payroll tax). It is the yield effect which, if significant, would lend critical support to the life cycle theory's conclusion that the social security system has reduced aggregate savings.

Finally, the remaining four studies in Table 10.1 made by Barro (1978), Barro and MacDonald (1979), Darby (1979), and Kopits and Gotur (1980) provide no support for the extended life cycle model.[22]

Barro (1978) uses the same consumption function used by Feldstein in 1974, but he includes a variable for the unemployment rate; then, the estimates of the coefficient of the social security wealth variable become both inconsistent and insignificant.

Darby (1979) uses his Consumer Expenditure Function[23] but instead of disposable income (used by Feldstein and Barro) he uses permanent income and transitory income; also, he uses variables for real money balances, interest rates, and relative prices. The results are that for the 1929-1974 time period the regressions indicate a 25 to 30 percent reduction in the saving-income ratio, whereas for the 1947-1974 time period, the effect is essentially nil or even an increase.

As far as the cross-country studies are concerned, by Barro and MacDonald (1979) and Kopits and Gotur (1980), they indicate that there is no support for the proposition that social security depresses private saving. Stated in other words this means that the wealth effect offsets the retirement effect. But it should be noted that the Kopits and Gotur study found that negative saving effects increased with the age of social security systems.

What then can be concluded about the effects of public pension systems on personal saving?[24] The null hypothesis of no significant impact is rejected in some studies which find important negative effects, but it cannot be rejected in others. Nevertheless, it seems that there is clearly a risk that pay-as-you-go pension systems might affect personal saving when such systems reach their maturity period.

From a technical point of view, it might be argued that time-series estimation of single-equation consumption functions involves simultaneity problems that inevitably call into question the reliability of the estimates. To correct this deficiency, we estimate, in Chapter 12, a long-run consumption function within a system of simultaneous equations which form a long-run model of the American economy; the theoretical foundations of this model are discussed in the next chapter. Moreover, in our estimation procedure we

will replace Feldstein's social security wealth variable by the new variable that we constructed in Chapter
9.

Before leaving this chapter, however, we will
briefly consider the policy implications of findings
of adverse effects of public pension systems on
capital formation.

POLICY IMPLICATIONS OF CAPITAL DEFICIENCY

Those economists who advocate that the public
pension system has caused a substantial reduction in
the capital stock have advanced the proposal that the
pension system should be fully-funded; Feldstein is
prominent among those who hold the above view.

However, the capital deficiency argument is of
secondary importance in this case. The real issue is
the degree of capital accumulation in the economy;
this issue involves an evaluation of the relative
magnitudes of the real rate of interest, r, and the
growth rate of output, g, for the economy under
consideration. If it is $r < n$, then a public pension
system that reduces capital will improve economic
efficiency; this is the essence of Aaron's "social
insurance paradox".[25]   However, the proponents
of full funding of public pension systems have in mind
the more realistic case when $r > n$; in this case the
actual capital-labor ratio for the economy is below
the optimal capital-labor ratio (which applies when
$r = n$). The real reason, therefore, behind the
proposals for full funding of public pensions is that
the current capital stock is not considered as the
socially optimal one; but, then, any government
program financed by a tax on income could be used to
remedy this alleged problem. Moreover, the fact that
r is greater than n does not imply that the allocation
of resources is inefficient; it simply means that
society has an amount of consumption per capita and
capital per capita which are lower than their respective values in the Golden Rule steady state.[26]   In
such a situation, there is no justification for an
increased rate of saving by means of fully funded
public pension systems, or by any other means, since
this extra saving would imply lower consumption by
the generations living in the transitional period
before the Golden Rule steady state is reached. A
decision to increase the rate of saving requires
judgments about the social rate of time preference
(for which there are no simple guidelines), and in any
case such a decision should not be based on a comparison of two steady-state levels of consumption; that
is, differences between steady states should not be

112

confused with changes from one steady state to another.
Finally, we should note that this brief discussion
has neglected the problems that would arise from
trying to transform large amounts of extra trust funds
into physical capital formation.[27]
We may conclude that the argument for increased
public savings is independent of the argument for
public pensions. Their essential difference is that
a public pension system is concerned with the intergenerational distribution of command over goods in a
given period, whereas a public savings plan is concerned with the intertemporal distribution of consumption.

NOTES

1. Referring to the American economy, Feldstein,
among others, has argued that capital formation has
been deficient as this is evidenced from the discrepancy between the risk-adjusted before-tax return on
investment and the after-tax return on saving;   see
Martin Feldstein, "National Saving in the United
States" in Capital for Productivity and Jobs,   The
American Assembly (Englewood Cliffs, N.J.: Prentice
Hall, 1977), pp. 124-154, and idem, "Does the United
States Save too Little?" American Economic Review,
Papers and Proceedings, Vol. 67, No. 1, February 1977,
pp. 116-121. On the other hand, other economists do
not find any evidence of inadequate capital formation
for the U.S. economy. See, among others, Richard
Musgrave, "Tax Policy and Capital Formation," National
Tax Journal, Vol. 32, No. 3, September 1979, pp. 351-
357, and Robert Elsner, "Capital Shortage: Myth and
Reality", American Economic Review, Papers and
Proceedings, Vol. 67, No. 1, February 1977, pp. 110-
115. However, Musgrave admits that more capital may
be required for the near future and, therefore,
appropriate measures should be taken.
2. Such limiting factors may be: the taxation
system, the structure of various transfer programs,
the size of government purchases, the tax-money-bond
mix of financing government expenditures, and efficiency of public investments. See George M. von
Furstenberg and Burton C. Malkiel, "The Government and
Capital Formation: A Survey of Recent Issues",
Journal of Economic Literature, Vol. 15, No. 5, Sept.
1977, pp. 835-878.
3. Feldstein is not explicit on this methodological point, but this is implicit in his article: "Do
Private Pensions Increase National Savings?", Journal

of Public Economics, Vol. 10, December 1978, pp. 277-293.

4. Ibid., pp. 284-285.

5. These cases are: (1) the favorable tax treatment of pension contributions and pension fund income, which raises the net rate of return that is available to workers; (2) the substitution of annuities for conventional retirement dissaving for the majority of workers; (3) the extent to which the change in retirement is correctly anticipated by workers and taken into account in their saving decisions; (4) private pensions may force workers to accumulate more assets than they would otherwise choose to do; and (5) workers may have an incorrect perception of prospective pension benefits. See M. Feldstein, "Do Private Pensions..." Ibid., pp. 279-284.

6. There is some evidence that stock markets do recognize unfunded pension liabilities; see G.S. Oldfield, "Financial Aspects of the Private Pension System," Journal of Money, Credit, and Banking, Vol. 9, February 1977, pp. 48-54.

7. See Martin Feldstein. "Tax Incentives, Corporate Savings, and Capital Accumulation in the United States." Journal of Public Economics, Vol. 2, April 1973, pp. 159-171.

8. Cagan and Katona (see citations in Reference 14 below) found that those covered by private pension plans saved more than those not covered. Allicia Munnell analyzed a subsample of Cagan's data and found directly contradictory results; later work provided further support for the conclusion that future retirement benefits lead to reduced personal savings. See A. Munnell The Effect of Social Security on Personal Savings (Cambridge: Ballinger Publishing Co., 1974), Chapter 5, and Idem, "Private Pensions and Saving: New Evidence", Journal of Political Economy, Vol. 84, October 1976, pp. 1013-1032. Finally, Feldstein estimated an aggregate consumption function which included a variable measuring total wealth of private pensions. The coefficient of this variable was insignificant and this implies that private pensions do not affect aggregate saving. See M. Feldstein, "Do Private Pensions...", Ibid., pp. 287-292.

9. See Martin Feldstein, "Social Security and Saving: The Extended Life Cycle Theory", American Economic Review, Papers and Proceedings, Vol. 66, May 1976, pp. 77-86.

10. See R.C. Hemming, "The Effect of State and Private Pensions on Retirement Behavior and Personal Capital Accumulation", Review of Economic Studies, Vol. 44, 1977, pp. 169-172, and Idem, "State Pensions and Personal Savings," Scottish Journal of Political

114

Economy, Vol. 25, No. 2, June 1978, pp. 135-148; S.C.
Hu, "On the Dynamic Behavior of the Consumer and the
Optimal Provision of Social Security," Review of
Economics and Statistics, Vol. XVL(3), No. 141, October
1978, pp. 437-446; L.J. Kotlikoff, "Social Security
and Equilibrium Capital Intensity", Quarterly Journal
of Economics, Vol. 93, May 1979, pp. 233-253, and Idem,
"Testing the Theory of Social Security and Life Cycle
Accumulation," American Economic Review, Vol. 69, June
1979, pp. 396-410.
    11. See L.J. Kotlikoff, "Testing the Theory of
Social Security..." Ibid., pp. 404.
    12. R. Barro, "Are Government Bonds Net Wealth?",
Journal of Political Economy, Vol. 82, Nov./Dec. 1974,
pp. 1095-1117.
    13. See T.W. Mirer, "The Wealth-Age Relations
among the Aged," American Economic Review, Vol. 69, No.
3, June 1979, pp. 435-443, and Michael R. Darby, The
Effects of Social Security on Income and the Capital
Stock, (Washington, D.C.: American Enterprise Institute, 1979), Chapter 3.
    14. See Phillip Cagan, The Effect of Pension Plans
on Aggregate Savings (National Bureau of Economic
Research, 1965), and George Katona, Private Pensions
and Individual Saving, (Survey Research Center, Univer-
sity of Michigan, 1965).
    15. See T.F. Pogue and L.G. Sgontz, "Social
Security and Investment in Human Capital." National
Tax Journal, Vol. 30, June 1977, pp. 157-169.
    16. This table is taken from: George F. Break,
"The Economic Effects of Social Security's OASI
Program." Mimeograph. (University of California,
Berkeley, March 1980), pp. 32-33.
    17. Martin Feldstein, "Social Security, Induced
Retirement..." (1974).
    18. See Martin Feldstein, "Discussion", Social
Security Bulletin, Vol. 42, No. 5, May 1979, pp. 36-39.
    19. See George F. Break, "The Economic Effects of
Social Security..." Ibid, p. 34.
    20. Martin Feldstein, "Social Security, Induced
Retirement..." (1974); Idem, "Social Security and
Private Savings: International Evidence in an Extended
Life Cycle Model" in M. Feldstein and R. Inman,
editors, The Economics of Public Services, Internation-
al Economic Association Series, 1977, Chapter 8; Idem,
"The Effect of Social Security..." (1979a); Idem, The
Effect of Social Security on Saving, National Bureau
of Economic Research, Working Paper 334, April (1979b);
Idem, Government Deficits and Aggregate Demand, Nation-
al Bureau of Economic Research, Working Paper 435,
January 1980; and Martin Feldstein and Anthony Pellechio, "Social Security and Household Wealth Accumula-

tion: New Evidence", Review of Economics and Statistics,
Vol. 61, August 1979, pp. 361-368.
   21. L.J. Kotlikoff, "Social Security and Equilibrium..." (1979a); Idem, "Testing the Theory..." (1979
b). And Allicia Munnell, "The Impact of Social
Security on Personal Savings," National Tax Journal,
Vol. 27, December 1974, pp. 553-567.
   22. Robert J. Barro, The Impact of Social Security
on Private Saving: Evidence from the U.S. Time Series
(Washington, D.C.: American Enterprise Institute, 1978);
Robert J. Barro and Glenn M. MacDonald, "Social Security and Consumer Spending in an International Cross
Section." Journal of Public Economics, Vol. 11, June
1979, pp. 275-289; Michael R. Darby, The Effects of
Social Security on Income and the Capital Stock
(Washington, D.C.: American Enterprise Institute,
1979); George Kopits and Padma Gotur, "The Influence
of Social Security on Household Savings: A Cross-
Country Investigation", International Monetary Fund
Staff Papers, Vol. 27, March 1980.
   23. See Michael R. Darby, "The Consumer Expenditure Function", Explorations in Economic Research, Vol.
4, Winter-Spring 1977-1978, pp. 645-674.
   24. In addition to the studies mentioned above,
there are two other studies, for Canada and Sweden,
that attempt to estimate the impact of the respective
national pension systems on aggregate saving. See P.
Boyle and J. Murray, "Social Security Wealth and
Private Saving in Canada", Canadian Journal of Economics, Vol. 12, No. 3, August 1979, pp. 456-468; and
Ann-Charlotte Stahlberg, "Effects of the Swedish
Supplementary Pension System on Personal and Aggregate
Household Saving", Scandinavian Journal of Economics,
Vol. 82, 1980, pp. 25-44. The former study applies
Feldstein's model to Canadian data for 1954-75; the
study did not find any statistically significant
effect of the national pension system on saving. The
latter study shows that a fully-funded public pension
system would increase the national saving ratio by 50-
100 percent; on the other hand, simulations showed
that a pay-as-you-go pension system would reduce
personal savings.
   25. See Henry Aaron, "The Social Insurance
Paradox", Canadian Journal of Economics and Political
Science, Vol. 32, August 166, pp. 371-374.
   26. For a technical discussion of these issues
see: M. Kurz and M. Avrin, Current Issues of the U.S.
Pension System. Mimeograph. Paper Prepared for the
President's Commission on Pension Policy, June 1979,
pp. 135-163.
   27. The possibility of transforming extra pension
(trust) funds to physical capital formation is discus-

sed in <u>Funding Pensions: Issues and Implications for</u>
<u>Financial Markets</u>, The Federal Research Bank of Boston
Conference Series, No. 16, October 1976. See especial-
ly the following two articles in this volume for
suggestions to accumulate trust funds for the OASI
program and for government pension systems respective-
ly: M.S. Feldstein, "The Social Security Fund and
National Capital Accumulation", pp. 32-64; and A.
Munnell and Ann Connolly, "Funding government Pensions:
State-Local, Civil Service and Military", pp. 72-133.
How financial markets would absorb those funds was
discussed by Benjamin M. Friedman, "Public Pension
Funding and U.S. Capital Formation: A Medium Run
View", pp. 156-201. For comments by Modigliani and
Tobin see Ibid., pp. 201-212.

11
A Pay-As-You-Go Pension System
in a Steady-State Growth Model

We have argued that it is analytically convenient to view the short-run operation of a pay-as-you-go pension system as a tax-transfer mechanism, and to view the system's long-run operation as a government-imposed system of intergenerational transfers that is analogous to public debt issues.

The latter view of the pay-as-you-go pension system will permit us to use a model of long-run steady-state growth in order to analyze the impact of the pension system on capital formation. This model has been designed specifically to serve the purpose of analyzing the dynamic incidence of the national debt.[1] Our approach represents a major departure from the life-cycle models that were reviewed in the previous chapter.

As far as the economic principles of debt financing are concerned, the main question is whether debt financing (or pay-as-you-go financing of pensions) shifts the burden from present to future generations.[2] The answer is that the burden can be passed on to future generations, but only insofar as the present generation responds to the government's action by reducing its rate of saving. Concerning the issue of whether funds for debt finance will come out of consumption or investment, there is no general agreement among economists. Proponents of the so-called "tax-debt equivalence theorem" have argued that a dollar of tax reduction creates an extra dollar of national debt that must eventually be repaid or serviced by interest payments with the same present value; since there is no change in the present value of the tax liabilities, there should be no change in consumption.[3] Hence, there is only an ex ante or nominal crowding-out effect which will not have any impact on economic activity.[4] Opponents of this view argue that the assumptions underlying this argument are very strong; that is, the equivalence theorem would hold if (1) capital markets were perfect and (2) people expected to live for ever, paying known taxes,

117

or they treated the known liabilities of taxpayers in
the future as their own.[5]   According to the latter
view the incidence of public debt is on both consumption and investment; we will follow this approach.

Our model of economic growth will be used to
analyze the degree of crowding-out of private capital
due to the wealth effects of higher government indebtedness resulting from the operation of a pay-as-you-go
pension system. In growth models with proper scaling,
increasing debt per capita and the ratio of government
debt to GNP raises private wealth if the total capital
stock could be taken as fixed; this depends on the
difference between the rate of interest, r, and the
growth rate of real output, n.[6]   The result
remains conditional, however, upon the premise that an
increase in public debt causes little or no reduction
in the capital stock. But this premise is unaccepta-
ble in long-run analysis. It is likely that in the
long-run the net wealth effects of increasing debt
might be not only smaller than the gross wealth effects
but they may well be negative (due to the crowding-out
of private capital); the model developed in this
chapter is capable of analyzing the long-run relationship between a permanent change in public indebtedness
per capita and the resulting permanent change in
capital intensiveness.

The basic postulates of our model are those used
in the simple version of the neoclassical growth model.
A closed economy is postulated in which technological
progress is either absent entirely or purely labor-
augmenting. With labor input measured either in
natural or in augmented units, all variables are
scaled by employment and expressed as so much per head.
All variables such as output, investment, and the
stock of capital per head are defined net of depreci-
ation.

Assuming linear homogeneity, output per head, y,
is a function of capital per head, k:

$$y = f(k) \tag{1}$$

The production technology satisfies the regularity
conditions; that is, $f(k) > 0$, $f'(k) > 0$, $f''(k) < 0$ for
$0 < k < \infty$, while $f(o) = 0$, $f(\infty) = \infty$, and $f'(o) = \infty$,
$f'(\infty) = o$.

Output per capita, y, is divided into consumption
per capita, $c \geq o$, and investment per capita, $z \geq o$.
That is,

$$y = c + z = f(k) \tag{2}$$

In growth equilibrium all inputs and stocks must
be growing at the same fixed rate as labor inputs, or
n percent per year. Hence, private net investment
must equal n·k each year if the steady-state k is to
remain fixed.

Assuming further that government purchases of
goods and services amount to γ percent of y, the
supply of consumer goods per head, c_s, is obtained as
what remains after satisfying all government
claims[7] and private investment claims to the
total output:

$$c_s = (1 - \gamma) \cdot (y - nk) \qquad (3)$$

In equilibrium this supply must be equal to the
demand for privately purchased consumer goods, c_D.
Consumer demand per head, c_D, is a fixed fraction, $0 <
1 - s < 1$, of private disposable income which is here
comprised of rewards to privately owned factors and
government transfers less taxes. That is:

$$c_D = (1 - s) \cdot (y + \varphi) \qquad (4)$$

where φ is net government transfers per head and it is
defined as the difference between the deficit per
head, δ, and government expenditures per head, g. It
is assumed that government expenditures, $g = \gamma \cdot y$, are
financed by taxes exclusively, whereas the deficit is
created by the transfer payments for pensions of a pay-
as-you-go pension system. In a steady state debt per
capita, Δ, as any other stock, must remain constant;
hence, it must be: $\delta = n\Delta$.

Then we have:

$$\varphi = \delta - \gamma \cdot y \qquad (5)$$

and, therefore, (4) can be rewritten as follows:

$$c_D = (1 - s) \cdot ((1 - \gamma) \cdot y + n\Delta)) \qquad (4.1)$$

Of course, this framework may be extended to take
into account the need for additional or smaller amounts
of debt per capita than that required by the operation
of the pay-as-you-go pension system, according to the
requirements of the stabilizational policies.[8] In
either case the assumption of a constant steady-state
debt per capita may be satisfied either by using an
increasing part of the additional deficit spending for
interest payments or by increasing taxes to prevent
the total debt from growing faster than GNP.

If we restrict, as we do, our discussion to public

debt created by the operation of the pay-as-you-go
pension system, then it is easier to satisfy the
assumption of constant debt per capita, provided that
the pension system is a mature one. Indeed, as we may
see from equation (5) in Chapter 9, in a mature pay-as-
you-go pension system the annual deficit, which is
created because of the operation of the system, increases at a rate which is equal to the growth rate of
real average taxable earnings and the growth rate of
the labor force. But the sum of these two growth
rates is equal to the growth rate of real output for
the economy. Hence, the amount of debt per head is
constant. For this conclusion to hold, of course, the
contribution and benefit structures of the pay-as-you-
go pension system must have stabilized. This is unlikely to happen during the early years of operation of a
pension system; but this is not undesirable as we are
going to see below.

Going back now to equation (4.1) we observe that
this specification prejudices our results to show that
enlarged deficits must stimulate private consumption
demand and, at a given level of income, such consumption could rise only at the expense of private investment since γ is fixed. The reason for this bias lies
in our inability to determine what portion of the debt
comes out of consumption and what portion comes out of
investment. As we discussed at the beginning of this
chapter, increased debt has an adverse effect on
capital formation only if the funds for purchasing
debt come out of investment. If a pay-as-you-go
pension system did not exist, then the most likely
situation would be that a certain part of total
pensions annually, say 1-θ percent of total pensions,
would take the form of intrafamily transfers, and the
rest θ percent would come out of fully (or partially)
funded private pensions. Assuming that in both cases
(that is, with and without the pay-as-you-go pension
system) the total amount of pensions would be the
same, it is the portion θ of the required annual
deficit per head, nΔ, which is relevant in a discussion
of potential adverse effects of a pay-as-you-go pension
system on the degree of capital intensiveness across
steady states. Even the amount θ · n · Δ is an overestimate if private pensions are not fully funded.

Moreover, our discussion above assumes that households substitute public for private pensions at the
rate of one-to-one. However, across steady states the
marginal and average rate of substitution, ξ, may be
less or more than one. Assume that contributions to
a pay-as-you-go pension system yield a rate of return
equal to the growth rate of real output, n, and private
savings yield an after-tax real rate of return equal

to $(1-\gamma)\cdot r$ where γ is tax-financed government expenditures as a ratio of GNP, and r is real rate of interest. Then, if $(1-\gamma)\cdot r < n$, it is $\xi > 1$; and if $(1-\gamma)\cdot$ $\cdot r > n$, it is $\xi < 1$.
Equation (4.1) may now be rewritten as follows:

$$C_D = (1-s)\cdot((1-\gamma) \ y + \xi \cdot \theta \cdot n \cdot \Delta), \ 0 < \theta < 1. \quad (4.2)$$

Now we are ready to discuss balanced-growth solutions to the system of equations (1), (2), (3), and (4.2). In Figure 1, output per head, $f(k)$, and the nk-ray are plotted against the k-axis in the southeast quadrant. Also, from equation (3) we have $C_s = f(k) - \gamma f(k) - nk$; hence C_s is the difference between the nk and the $(1-\gamma) \cdot f(k)$ curves and it can be plotted against y in the northeast quadrant.
By setting the derivative of C_s with respect to k (see equation 3) equal to zero and noting that $f''(k) < 0$, it can readily be shown that private consumption reaches a maximum at the Golden Rule per capita output, $\hat{y}$, and the corresponding capital-labor ratio is $\hat{k}$. From the first-order condition we derive that in this equilibrium situation the after-tax rate of return, $(1-\gamma)r$, is equal to the growth rate, n.
The C_D function (equation 4.2) is a straight line with a slope equal to $(1-s)\cdot(1-\gamma)$. This function shifts with changes in the amount of debt per capita , Δ.
When $\Delta = 0$, we have the familirar Solow steady-state equilibrium where output per head is y* and capital per head is k*. This situation is shown by the consumption line C_D^0 in Figure 11.1. Given the structure of our model, a Solow steady state would be reached if the long-run debt per capita created by the pay-as-you-go pension system were offset completely by the long-run surplus per capita of the regular government budget. If the latter were greater than the former, then the long-run net position of the public sector would be positive and this would shift the C_D line downward in Figure 11.1. Output per capita would tend to reach $\hat{y}$, the maximum level of sustainable consumption. Beyond $\hat{y}$ the accumulation of capital would be inefficiently large, and in our model, expansion of the pay-as-you-go pension system could be used to increase efficiency in the allocation of resources; this could be done by increasing debt per capita of the pension system.
On the other hand, Δ may assume a maximum value, Δ^+, which is attained when the $C_D^!$ line is tangent to the C_s curve. In this case there is a unique equilibrium output per capita, y^+, and a capital-labor ratio, k^+. Moreover, by setting the partial derivatives with

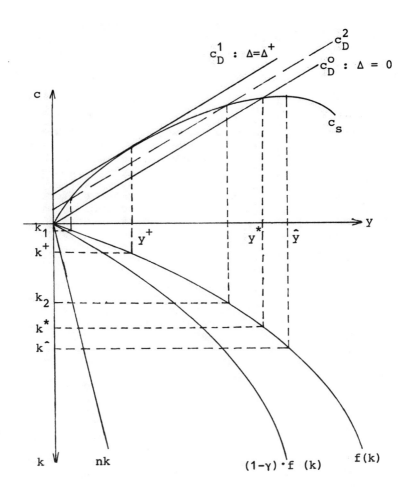

Figure 11.1
Dynamic Incidence of Public Debt

Source: E.S. Phelps and K. Shell, "Public Debt,
Taxation..." (1969).

respect to k equal for C_s (equation 3) and C_D (equation 4.2) we obtain the corresponding real rate for interest; it is $r = n/s \cdot (1 - \gamma)$.

In more realistic situations Δ will assume a value between zero and Δ^+. An intermediate case, where $0 < \Delta < \Delta^+$, is shown by line $C_D{}^2$ in Figure 11.1. Line $C_D{}^2$ intersects the C_s curve in two points, giving the corresponding capital-labor ratios k_1 and k_2. We may derive the general conclusion that for $\hat{y} > y > y^+$, an increase in the amount of debt per capita decreases the long-run output per capita. In the range $y^+ > y > 0$, an increase in the debt per capita increases output per capita.[9]

Furthermore, this model permits us to derive an important proposition in comparative dynamics. We want to know if government debt created by the pay-as-you-go pension sytem displaces private capital. To do that we equate C_D to C_s (equation 4.2 and 3, respectively) and then differentiate with respect to k.

We have :

$$C_D = C_s \longrightarrow (1-s) \cdot ((1-\gamma)y + \xi \cdot \theta \cdot n \cdot \Delta) =$$

$$= (1-\gamma) - nk \Longrightarrow (1-s) \cdot ((1-\gamma)y + \xi \cdot \theta \cdot n \cdot \Delta) -$$

$$- (1-\gamma)y + nk = 0$$

After differentiating and simplifying, we obtain:

$$\frac{\partial \Delta}{\partial k} = \frac{s(1 - \gamma) \cdot r - n}{(1 - s) \theta \cdot \xi \cdot n} \tag{5}$$

This relation shows that complete crowding out of private capital by government debt created by the pay-as-you-go pension system (that is, $\partial \Delta / \partial k = -1$) will occur if and only if the rate of interest is:

$$r_o = \frac{n (1 - (1 - S) \cdot \theta \cdot \xi)}{s (1 - \gamma)}$$

If $\theta = 1$, $\xi = 1$, then $r = n/(1 - \gamma)$; that is a dollar of debt created by the pay-as-you-go pension system displaces exactly one dollar of private capital only in the Golden Rule steady state. Furthermore, for $k < \hat{k}$, equation (5) shows that crowding out of private capital proceeds at a rate of more than one-to-one, since $(1 - \gamma)r > n$ requires that $\partial \Delta / \partial k > -1$ or $\partial k / \partial \Delta < -1$ or $- (\partial k / \partial \Delta) > 1$. The opposite is true in the inefficient region where $k > \hat{k}$.

However, it is more interesting to consider the general case, which is the main feature of our model, when $\theta \neq 1$ and $\xi \neq 1$, where θ measures the extent of

intrafamily transfers to retired members in the absence
of a public pension system, and ξ is the marginal and
average rate of substitution between private and public
pension benefits.

In this more general case, complete crowding out
takes place at such a level of capital intensiveness
where the real rate of return is given by r_o in equation (6). Hence we have to place r_o in relation
to r in Figure 11.1.

It can be shown easily that $r_o < \hat{r}$ if $\theta \cdot \xi > 1$.[10]
In this case complete crowding out of private capital
by the debt of the pension system (at the rate of one-
to-one) will take place at a steady state for which
$r = r_o < \hat{r}$. At any level of lower capital intensiveness crowding out will proceed at a rate greater than
one-to-one. Such a case would be possible if, for
example, $\theta = 0.50$ (which is a very plausible value)
and $\xi > 2$ (which is very likely to apply during the
period of expansion of a pay-as-you-go pension system).

On the other hand, it can be shown that $r_o > \hat{r}$ if
$\theta \cdot \xi < 1$. This case requires values of ξ in the range
0-1.9, assuming θ is around the value 0.50. Such
values for ξ are most likely to occur when a pay-as-you
-go pension system reaches its stage of maturity and
has a rate of return which is more or less equal to
that obtained in private investment alternatives. In
Figure 11.1, this case would be found in a steady state
with a capital-labor ratio greater than $\hat{k}$, because r_o
would then be greater than $\hat{r}$. Crowding out of private
capital at the rate of one-to-one would take place only
in this steady state. If r_o is close to r^+ in Figure
11.1, the implication of the above statement is that
for any steady state between k^+ (more accurately the k
that corresponds to r_o) and $\hat{k}$, crowding out of private
capital by debt of the pay-as-you-go pension system
would proceed, in the long-run at a rate of less than
one-to-one. Indeed, the range $(k^+, \hat{k})$ would include
capital-labor ratios that would seem applicable to most
industrial economies; it would be very unlikely for an
indistrial economy to be observed to operate outside
this range. For example, if the American economy can
be approximated with the values of $s = 0.08$, $\gamma = 0.22$,
and $n = 0.035$ (where s is net private savings rate, γ
is government exhaustive expenditure as a percentage of
GNP, and n is the growth rate of output), then $\hat{r} = 4.48$
percent and $r^+ = 56$ percent; this is definitely the
range within which the American economy operates.

We may use the ideas developed above to make some
crude calculations of the impact of the pay-as-you-go
pension system on the rate of savings and capital
formation for the American economy during the period
1950-1978. The estimates are shown on Table 11.1.

In Column 1 we list five possible steady states. Each
steady state is represented by its own interest rate
and the respective (assumed) values of ξ and θ. The
first steady state (line 1) is of special importance;
in this case the interest rate is calculated on the
basis of equation (6) for θ = 0.5 and ξ = 1.5. If the
values of θ and ξ are good approximations of the real
values, then in this steady state there will be
complete crowding-out of private capital at the rate
of one-to-one. As we showed earlier, any other steady
state with a higher capital-labor ratio will be associated with crowding-out effects of less than one-to-
one. We will consider two such steady states; one
with an interest rate equal to 12 percent (because
this is the rate of return on corporate capital in the
U.S. for the period 1950-1978[11]) and the other with
an interest rate equal to 4.48 percent, which is the
case of the Golden Rule steady state.

The values in column 2 are calculated on the
basis of equation (5) by using the values of θ and ξ
shown in column 1 for the respective steady state.
The values in column 3 are the reciprocals of those
in column 2. The values in Column 3 are consistent
with our analysis, that is, they show that crowding
out of private capital by the debt of the pay-as-you-
go pension system is less than one-to-one. The values
found in column 3 are used in columns 4 and 5 to
estimate how much capital was displaced during the
period 1950-1978 because of the debt of the pension
system. For this period, the average debt per capita
was 0.35 (or 350 dollars at 1972 prices); this value
is obtained when the average social security wealth
for m = 30, from Table 9.1 of Chapter 9, is divided by
the total population (descriptions and sources of
variables are given in Appendix D). The values in
column 4 are derived by multiplying the values of
column 3 by D = 0.35, where D is the amount of debt
per capita created by the OASI program. Moreover,
during the period 1950-1978, the amount of capital per
capita was 9.3 (or 9.300 dollars at 1972 prices). The
values in column 5 are derived by dividing the values
of column 4 by 9.3 and expressing the result in percentage terms.

We should note that the results shown in column 5
depend on the validity of the assumptions we made
above. In all cases shown on Table 11.1, the estimated
reduction in capital per capita because of the debt per
capita created by the OASI program is small. However,
the qualitative conclusions of the model are confirmed;
that is, if the amount of debt per capita is permanent-
ly increased, then the economy will, in the long run
reach another steady state with a lower ratio of
capital per capita. This qualitiative conclusion was

TABLE 11.1
Estimated Crowding-out of Private Capital by the Debt of the OASI Program

	1	2	3	4	5
	Description of Steady State	$\frac{\partial \Delta}{\partial K}$	$\frac{\partial K}{\partial \Delta} = \frac{1}{\partial \Delta / \partial k}$	(3) · D where: D = 0.35	Estimated Reduction in Capital per capita
1.	17.4% ($\theta = 0.5$) ($\Xi = 1.5$)	-1.00	-1	-0.350	3.7%
2.	12% ($\theta = 0.5$),($\Xi = 1.5$)	-1.55	-0.64	-0.224	2.4%
3.	12% ($\theta = 0.5$),($\Xi = 1.5$)	-1.14	-0.88	-0.308	3.3%
4.	4.48% ($\theta = 0.5$),($\Xi = 1.1$)	-1.82	-0.55	-0.193	2.1%
5.	4.48% ($\theta = 0.5$),($\Xi = 1.5$)	-1.33	-0.75	-0.263	2.8%

Note: For explanation of symbols see text.

the main objective of this chapter. In the following
chapter we will use more formal quantitative methods
to estimate the impact of the OASI program on the
American economy.

NOTES

1. Our model is an adaptation of a model developed by Edmund Phelps and Karl Shell in 1969 to analyze
the impact of government deficits on capital intensiveness in the long run. See E.S. Phelps and K. Shell,
"Public Debt, Taxation, and Capital Intensiveness",
Journal of Economic Theory, Vol. 1, No. 3, October
1969, pp. 330-346.
2. The burden of the national debt has been one
of the most debated issues in the economic leterature.
The argument against is summarized in Abba P. Lerner,
"The Burden of the National Debt" in Income, Employment
and Public Policy: Essays in Honor of Alvin H. Hansen,
edited by L.A. Metzler (New York: Norton Publishing
Co., 1948), pp. 255-261. The argument for is contain-
ed in W.G. Bowen, R.G. Davis and D.H. Kopt, "The
Public Debt: A Burden on Future Generations?"
American Economic Review, Vol. 50, 1960, pp. 701-706.
An evaluation of all arguments and the final verdict
are included in Carl S. Shoup, "Debt Financing and
Future Generations", Economic Journal, Vol. 72, 1962,
pp. 887-898. Our discussion follows the last source.
3. Some recent works in support of the equivalence
theorem are: Martin J. Bailey, National Income and
the Price Level (New York: McGraw Hill, 1971), especi-
ally Chapter 10; R. Barro, "Are Government Bonds Net
Wealth?" Journal of Political Economy, Vol. 82, No. 6,
Nov./Dec. 1974, pp. 1095-1117; P.A. David and J.L.
Scadding, "Private Savings: Ultrarationality, Aggre-
gation, and Denison's Law", Journal of Political
Economy, Vol. 82, March/April 1974, pp. 225-249; L
Kochin, "Are Future Taxes Anticipated by Consumers?"
Journal of Money, Credit and Banking August 1974, Vol.
6, pp. 385-394; J.E. Tanner, "Fiscal Policy and
Consumer Behavior", Review of Economics and Statistics,
Vol. LXI, No. 2, May 1979, pp. 317-321, and J.E.
Tanner, "An Empirical Test of the Extent of Tax Dis-
countings A Comment" Journal of Money, Credit and
Banking, May 1979, Vol. 11, pp. 214-218.
4. For a taxonomy of crowding-out effects see
Willem H. Buiter, "Crowding Out and the Effectiveness
of Fiscal Policy", Journal of Public Economics, Vol. 7,
1977, pp. 309-328.

5. This is an old argument but for a recent restatement see Martin Feldstein, Government Deficits and Aggregate Demand, National Bureau of Economic Research, Working Paper No. 435, January 1980, pp. 6-9.

6. If $r < n$, then a debt issue would be regarded as net wealth. If $r > n$, then an extra amount of taxes of $(r - n) \cdot \Delta$, where Δ is debt per head, would be required in order to limit the growth of the government debt. But even in this case private wealth will be somewhat increased because individuals will fail to discount completely their future tax liabilities, unless they are "ultrarational". For a discussion of these issues see: Martin Feldstein, "Perceived Wealth in Bonds and Social Security: A Comment," Journal of Political Economy, Vol. 84, No. 2, April 1976, pp. 331-336, and Robert Barro "Reply to Feldstein and Buchanan", Journal of Political Economy, Vol. 84, No. 2, April 1976, pp. 343-349. See, also, Earl Thompson, "Debt Instruments in Macroeconomic and Capital Theory", American Economic Review, Vol. 57, No. 5, December 1967, pp. 1196-1210.

7. The conventional but generally quite unjustified assumption is made here that the government wastes γ percent of all resources. For a study that attempts to remedy this analytical shortcoming see: George M. von Furstenberg, "The Effect of the Changing Size and Composition of Government Purchases on Potential Output," Review of Economics and Statistics, Vol. LXII, No. 1, Febr. 1980, pp. 74-80.

8. Presumably the total amount of debt (that is the total sum of regular debt issued for stabilization purposes and the implicit debt issued for the obligations of the pay-as-you-go pension system) cannot exceed an upper limit, which is determined by the structure of the economy. The maximum debt-output ratio must be equal to a/λ, where λ is the constant rate of growth of money national income, and "a" is the deficit as a proportion of national income and it can be shown to be constant over time. See E. Donar, "The Burden of Debt and the National Income", American Economic Review, Vol. 34, December 1944, pp. 798-827.

9. A dynamic analysis of the model will show that the equilibrium situations found in Figure 11 are stable in the region $(y^+, \bar{y})$, whereas they are unstable in the region $(0, y^+)$. See: E.S. Phelps and K. Shell, "Public Debt..." (1969), pp. 340-343. The instability in the latter case is due to the requirement of constant debt per capita across steady states. This problem could be overcome in economies with low capital-labor ratios by the introduction of a pay-as-you-go pension system with a small amount of debt per capita initially, which could be increased later as the economy reached higher levels of capital intensiveness.

10. If we subtract $\hat{r} = n/(1-\gamma)$ from r_o (equation 6), we will find: $n(1 - s)(1 - \theta\xi)/s(1-\gamma)$. This is negative, indicating $r_o < \hat{r}$, if $\theta\xi > 1$.

11. See Martin Feldstein and Lawrence Summers, "Is the Rate of Profit Falling?" <u>Brookings Papers in Economic Activity</u>, Vol. 1, 1977, pp. 211-227.

12
The Impact of a Pay-As-You-Go Pension System on Income and the Capital Stock: Evidence from the U.S. Time Series

In this chapter we will employ concepts and
theories developed in earlier chapters of Part 3 to
analyze the issue of whether and by how much social
security has reduced (or increased) the capital stock
in the United States.

Previous work, based on U.S. aggregate time series
data, has involved estimation of consumption (or
saving) functions. The time series regressions, however, have been inconclusive (an extensive survey of
the literature is given in Chapter 10). Feldstein
estimated a 37 percent reduction in the private saving-
income ratio. Alicia Munnell estimated a reduction of
only 5 percent, whereas Barro obtained no evidence of
any reduction. Darby found that, taken as a whole, his
evidence suggests that the saving-income ratio may have
been reduced anywhere from 0 to 25 percent, although
the range from 0 to 10 percent appears most probable.

All the studies mentioned above follow a common
methodology. They use some type of consumption
function which is extended to include the social security wealth variable of Feldstein.[1] However, as we
argued in Chapter 9, Feldstein's social security wealth
variable is not the appropriate measure of the wealth
that is generated by the operation of the pay-as-you-go
pension system. Instead, we suggested a new way of
constructing a social security wealth variable. In
this chapter we will use the social security wealth
variable we constructed in Chapter 9 in order to
measure the impact of the U.S. OASI program on the
saving-income ratio.

In the first section of this chapter we incorpo-
rate our social security wealth variable into the
extended consumption functions of Feldstein, Barro, and
Darby and we reestimate these functions by using
standard regression techniques.

Unfortunately, time-series estimation of single-
equation consumption functions involves simultaneity
problems that inevitably call into question the relia-

bility of the estimates. Therefore, in the second section of this chapter we undertake the econometric estimation of a simultaneous system of long-run behavioral functions; one among them is a long-run consumption function which is extended to include the social security wealth variable, in the form of extra public debt, that we developed in Chapter 9. The estimated model is then used to estimate, by employing a simulation analysis, the effect of the U.S. OASI program on the capital stock and the rate of economic growth.

In the final section of this chapter we present our overall conclusions on the potential impact of the U.S. OASI program on the American economy.

ESTIMATES BASED ON CONSUMPTION FUNCTIONS

In this section we will reestimate the consumption functions used by Feldstein, Barro, and Darby to analyze the effects of the social security system.[2] The new element in this analysis is that we replace Feldstein's social security wealth variable by the public-debt-like social security wealth variable that we developed in Chapter 9.

Feldstein employed his Extended Consumption Function which is an extension of the 1963 Ando-Modigliani consumption function.[3]   The mathematical specification of this consumption function is:

$$C_t = a_o + a_1 Y_t + a_2 RE_t + a_3 Y_{t-1} + a_4 U_t + a_5 W_{t-1} + a_6 SSW_t$$

where: C_t = consumer expenditures
         Y_t = disposable personal income
         RE_t = gross business retained earnings
         U_t = unemployment rate
         W_t = market value of privately owned wealth
         SSW_t = social security wealth

The function above was estimated for data from 1946 through 1978. All variables except U_t were measured in 1972 dollars per capita.[4] It should be noted that in the estimated equations the unemployment variable is specified as changing the marginal propensity to consume (that is, as a multiplier of Y_t) rather than as a separate linear term; the new variable is UYD.[5]

The expected signs of the coefficients are (a_1, a_2, a_3, a_4, a_5) > 0. The hypothesis to be tested is that a_6 = 0, rather than a_6 > 0. The estimated

TABLE 12.1
Estimates of the Extended Consumption Function

| Regression Number | Constant | Y_t | Estimated Coefficient Of | | | UYD_t | SSW_t | R^2 and D - W |
			Y_{t-1}	RE_t	W_{t-1}			
1	514.2 (3.74)	0.674 (11.0)	-0.0268 (1.44)	0.0739 (.49)	0.0161 (2.46)	-0.0605 (0.36)	0.5192 (1.35)	.9983 D.W. = 1.58
2	---	0.890 (36.0)	-0.0226 (1.0)	0.2810 (1.68)	0.0173 (2.17)	-0.1150 (0.57)	-0.7280 (3.12)	.9973 D.W. = 1.70
3	530.9 (3.55)	0.650 (9.8)	0.0010 (0.062)	0.0749 (0.46)	---	0.2040 (1.47)	1.004 (2.79)	.9978 D.W. = 1.16
4	---	0.872 (35.2)	0.0075 (0.39)	0.289 (1.62)	---	0.1681 (1.02)	-0.2491 (3.01)	.9968 D.W. = 1.26
5	514.8 (3.38)	0.661 (9.9)	0.0014 (0.086)	0.096 (0.58)	---	---	1.011 (2.75)	.9977 D.W. = 1.05
6	---	0.875 (35.8)	0.0077 (0.40)	0.302 (1.69)	---	---	-0.2114 (2.85)	.9967 D.W. = 1.10

Note: The parentheses below the coefficient estimates give t-statistics.

coefficients of the respective variables are shown in
Table 12.1. Feldstein's favorite specification is the
first regression in the table. It may be seen at once
that the y_{t-1} and UYD_t variables have the opposite than
the expected signs. Successive changes in the specification of the consumption function showed that this
was due to the presence of the wealth variable (this is
so even when the SSW variable is entirely deleted).
   Another important observation is that the SSW
variable changes signs consistently depending on the
presence or absence of the constant term. Whenever
the constant term is absent, the SSW variable assumes
a negative sign. As we are going to discuss below,
Barro has made the argument that due to simultaneity
problems (and assuming that the household utility
functions are homothetic) the constant term should be
excluded from a linear specification of the consumption
function. If this were correct, then we will have to
conclude that the social security system has had a
positive influence on the saving-income ratio, and
therefore has contributed to more capital formation.
   In any case, we believe that none of the regressions in Table 12.1 is statistically acceptable for
the purpose of deriving any conclusions concerning the
influence of the social security system on saving and
the capital stock.
   Robert Barro's time series analysis of the effects
of social security on the saving-income ratio is based
on a consumer expenditure function which is extended
to include the social security wealth variable.[6] His
proxies for permanent and transitory income are similar
to the variables used by Feldstein, in his earlier
studies, but in addition Barro included an unemployment
rate variable.
   The mathematical specification of the consumer
expenditure function used by Barro is:

$$C_t = a_0 + a_1 YD_t + a_2 YD_{t-1} + a_3 RE_t + a_4 SUR_t +$$

$$+ a_5 UYD_t + a_6 K_t + a_7 DUR_t + a_8 SSW_t$$

where :
C_t = consumer expenditure
YD_t = disposable personal income
RE_t = (net) corporate retained earnings
SUR_t = surplus of the total government sector
UYD_t = U · UD; where U is the unemployment rate
K_t = net stocks of fixed nonresidential business capital and net stocks of nongovern-
mental residential housing at the beginning of the year

DUR_t = net stocks of household durables, exclusive of housing, at the beginning of the year

SSW_t = social security wealth.

The consumer expenditure function was estimated for data from 1946 through 1974. All variables except the unemployment rate are expressed in 1958 dollars per capita.[7]

The expected signs[8] of the coefficients are $(a_1, a_2, a_3, a_4, a_5, a_6) > 0$, $a_7 < 0$. The key hypothesis to be tested is that $a_8 = 0$, rhather than $a_8 > 0$. Table 12.2 shows that all variables have the expected signs with the exception of the RE variable which has consistently the opposite sign and is statistically insignificant in all regressions.

Barro has made the argument that due to simultaneity problems and, to a lesser extent, due to the plausible assumption that the underlying household utility functions may be homothetic, the constant a_0 in the linear consumer expenditure function should be set equal to zero.[9] Regressions 2, 4, and 6 in Table 12.2 are estimated without the constant. The principal effect of deleting the constant is on the estimates of the two stock variables, K and DUR. For the durables variable, the deletion of the constant changes the estimated coefficient from an insignificant one to a significant one of plausible magnitude. The same effect takes place with respect to the coefficient of the capital variable, K. It seems then that more reliance should be placed on the regressions in Table 12.2 in which the constant is absent.

Feldstein has criticized Barro for using the government surplus, SUR, variable.[10] Feldstein considers SUR as an endogenous variable. Regressions 5 and 6 in Table 12.2 show how the coefficients are altered when the SUR variable is deleted.

As far as the SSW variable is concerned, we see from regressions 2, 4, and 6 that the relative range of the magnitude of the coefficients is between 0.5 and 0.7. In all cases the coefficients are significant at the 5 percent level of statistical significance. It should be mentioned that Feldstein's SSW variable was always insignificant and/or had the "wrong" sign in regressions identical to those shown in Table 12.2.

The estimated percentage reduction in the 1972 saving-income ratio is about 26 to 33 percent (these values correspond to the minimum 0.5 and the maximum 0.7 coefficients found above). These estimates compare with a 37 percent reduction found by Martin Feldstein when he used his own social security wealth variable, and his own consumption function specification.

TABLE 12.2
(Barro) Estimates of the Extended Consumer Expenditure Function

Regression Number	Constant	YD_t	YD_{t-1}	RE_t	Estimated Coefficient Of SUR_t	UYD_t	K_t	DUR_t	SSW_t	R^2 and D-W
1	150.556 (1.30)	0.818 (12.79)	0.039 (2.69)	-0.203 (1.44)	0.112 (1.39)		0.0237 (0.66)	-0.197 (1.50)	0.825 (2.56)	.9989 D.W. = 2.36
2	—	0.893 (29.92)	0.042 (2.89)	-0.191 (1.33)	0.133 (1.66)		0.0602 (2.65)	-0.320 (3.40)	0.608 (2.17)	.9988 D.W. = 2.50
3	141.781 (1.29)	0.826 (13.50)	0.040 (2.89)	-0.105 (0.71)	0.135 (1.73)	0.289 (1.75)	0.0105 (0.30)	-0.172 (1.37)	0.715 (2.28)	.9991 D.W. = 2.44
4	—	0.896 (31.42)	0.043 (3.09)	-0.090 (0.64)	0.156 (2.00)	0.289 (1.78)	0.0444 (1.89)	-0.287 (3.14)	0.507 (1.85)	.9990 D.W. = 2.55
5	189.90 (1.60)	0.829 (12.96)	0.045 (3.23)	-0.194 (1.35)		0.240 (1.41)	0.00049 (.013)	-0.200 (1.53)	0.933 (3.10)	.9989 D.W. = 2.37
6	—	0.923 (34.56)	0.050 (3.55)	-0.193 (1.30)		0.244 (1.38)	0.0435 (1.74)	-0.358 (3.99)	0.700 (2.57)	.9988 D.W. = 2.42

Note: The parentheses below the coefficient estimates give t-statistics.

For the year 1958 the estimated reduction in the saving-income ratio due to the operation of the social security system was in the range from 19 percent to 24 percent.[11]

Michael Darby used his own consumer expenditure function (see Note 6). In this function consumer expenditures appear to be explained by four principal factors: permanent income (the normal income stream from total human and nonhuman wealth), transitory income (the difference between current and permanent income), excess money supply, and the stock of consumers' durable goods. As was mentioned earlier Barro also used this type of consumption function but he employed different proxies for permanent and transitory income.

Darby's complete mathematical specification of the consumer expenditure function is:

$$C_t = a_0 + a_1\ YP_t + a_2\ YT_t + a_3\ M_t + a_4\ D_{t-1} + a_5\ RP_t +$$

$$+ a_6\ RR_t + a_7\ SSW_t$$

where :

C_t = consumer expenditures
YP_t = permanent income
YT_t = transitory income
M_t = real money balances
D_t = the stock of consumers' durable goods at the end of the year
RP_t = the ratio of the prices of durable and nondurable good
RR_t = the market interest rate
SSW_t = social security wealth.

All variables except RP_t and RR_t are measured in billions of 1958 dollars.[12] The expected signs of the coefficients are: $(a_1,\ a_2,\ a_3,\ a_5) > 0$, and $(a_4,\ a_5) < 0$. The hypothesis to be tested is that $a_7 = 0$, rather than $a_7 > 0$.

The expanded consumer expenditure function is estimated for data from 1946 through 1974. The estimated coefficients are shown in Table 12.3. All coefficients have the expected signs, with the exception of the RP_t variable which is not statistically significant in any of the regressions, and its sign is sensitive to the specification of the consumption function.

As far as the impact of the social security system on the saving-income ratio is concerned, our regressions show that we cannot reject the hypothesis that the social security wealth variable is not significantly different from zero in either a statistical or an economic sense. This result does not change even after we respecify the consumption function, as regressions

TABLE 12.3
(Darby) Estimates of the Extended Consumer Expenditure Function

Regression Number	Constant	YP_t	YT_t	Estimated Coefficient Of M_t	D_{t-1}	RP_t	RR_t	SSW_t	R^2 and D-W
1	-55.79 (1.00)	0.884 (17.2)	0.522 (9.04)	0.348 (2.99)	-0.118 (3.18)	4.94 (0.11)	1.35 (0.78)	0.150 (0.56)	.995 D-W = 2.32
2	---	0.860 (18.85)	0.522 (9.03)	0.304 (2.81)	-0.125 (3.45)	-35.7 (2.70)	1.64 (0.96)	0.123 (0.46)	.996 D-W = 2.26
3	4.30 (0.07)	0.897 (15.04)	0.591 (9.53)		-0.164 (4.10)	-8.39 (0.17)	1.95 (0.98)	0.412 (1.40)	.9994 D-W = 2.09
4	-49.68 (2.96)	0.882 (18.9)	0.522 (9.28)	0.347 (3.07)	-0.119 (3.33)		1.37 (0.82)	0.140 (0.57)	.9996 D-W = 2.32
5	-62.90 (1.18)	0.899 (19.1)	0.509 (9.32)	0.359 (3.14)	-0.117 (3.17)	9.24 (0.22)		0.163 (0.62)	.9995 D-W = 2.23
6	-6.63 (0.68)	0.920 (18.37)	0.574 (10.06)		-0.163 (4.23)			0.449 (1.69)	.9994 D-2 = 1.93

Note : The parentheses below the coefficient estimates give t-statistics.

2, 3, 4, 5, and 6 in Table 12.3 show. Darby, using
Feldstein's social security wealth variable, found
similar results except in the case when the sample
period was extended back to 1929: in the latter case
the coefficient of the SSW variable was significant at
the 10 percent level of statistical significance.

ESTIMATES BASED ON A SYSTEM OF SIMULTANEOUS EQUATIONS

The estimates reported in the previous section
are all based on ordinary least squares. This estimation procedure has familiar desirable properties,
but is also subject to well-known simultaneity problems
which arise from the likely correlation between shifts
in the consumption function and some of the explanatory
variables. It is remarkable that none of the studies
that have been made so far, to measure the impact of
the social security system on saving and capital formation, has employed a general equilibrium framework.
   In this section we will try to estimate the effect
of the U.S. OASI program on the capital stock and the
rate of economic growth, for the period 1946-1978, by
using a simultaneous system of equations that represent, in an aggregate sense, a description of the
structure of the American economy. More specifically,
we use as the basis of our analysis the Morishina-Saito
log-linear macroeconomic model for the American
economy.[13]   This is a model of the Keynesian type
and consists of six stochastic and two definitional
equations.
   Our analysis will proceed at two stages. At the
first stage the simultaneously determined consumption
function will be used, as a first approximation, to
estimate the impact of the operation of the OASI program on saving. At the second stage the simultaneous
equations will be transformed into a model of long-run
economic growth which will be used as the basis for a
simulation, the basic purpose of which will be to
determine the effect of an increased steady-state debt
per capita on capital formation. The theoretical basis
of this analysis is that of Chapter 11. In other
words, this section is the quantitative extension of
the theoretical discussion of Chapter 11.
   The Morishima-Saito annual model was estimated by
the method of two-stage-least-squares over the sample
period 1946-1978. A list of the variables follows.
   The endogenous variables:

Y = net national product (billions of 1972
    dollars)
C = consumption (billions of 1972 dollars)

K = end of year capital stock (billions of 1972 dollars)
N = persons actually employed (millions of persons)
P = price level (1972 base: 1)
W = wage rate (thousands of current dollars)
r = corporate bond yield (percent per annum)
h = hours worked per person per year (thousands of hours).

The exogenous variables:

I = net investment (billions of 1972 dollars)
B = trade balance (billions of 1972 dollars)
M = cash balances (billions of current dollars)
L = population sixteen years of age and over (millions of persons)
t = time in years (1962: 0)
U = dummy variable (0 before 1950)
D = total government debt, including social-security-created debt (billions of 1972 dollars)
CAP = capacity utilization rate in manufacturing (percent).

A more exact description of the variables and the sources for the respective variables are given in Appendix D.

The estimated equations as well as the two iden- tities are given below.[14]

1. The Consumption Function

$$\log \frac{C_t}{L_t} = \underset{(3.61)}{-0.727} + \underset{(8.3)}{0.797} \log \frac{Y_t}{L_t} + \underset{(3.03)}{0.301} \log \frac{M_t}{P_t \cdot L_t} +$$

$$+ \underset{(3.8)}{0.116} \log \frac{C_{t-1}}{L_{t-1}} + \underset{(1.56)}{0.158} \log \frac{D_t}{L_t}$$

$$R^2 = .9870 , \qquad D\text{-}W = .577$$

2. The Liquidity Preference Function

$$\log \frac{M_t}{P_t} = \underset{(2.8)}{-1.03} + \underset{(2.9)}{0.154} \log Y_t + \underset{(15.5)}{1.03} \log \frac{M_{t-1}}{P_t} -$$

$$\underset{(1.7)}{-0.074} \log r_t$$

$$R^2 = .9950 , \qquad D\text{-}W = 1.979$$

3. The Production Function

$$\log Y_t = 1.121 + 0.751 \log h_t N_t + 0.249 \log K_t +$$
$$(2.3)$$

$$0.00625t + 0.02282U$$
$$(2.7) \qquad (1.9)$$

$$R^2 = .9845 \ , \qquad D\text{-}W = .640$$

4. The Relative Share Equation

$$\frac{W_t N_t}{P_t Y_t} = .751 \Rightarrow \log \frac{W_t N_t}{P_t Y_t} = -0.1243$$
$$(1.10)$$

5. The Wage Determination Equation

$$\log \frac{W_t}{h_t} = 0.079 + 0.992 \log \frac{W_{t-1}}{h_{t-1}} +$$
$$(4.5) \quad (116.9)$$

$$+ 0.217 (\frac{1}{5} \log \frac{P_t}{P_{t-1}} + \frac{4}{5} \log \frac{P_{t-1}}{P_{t-2}}) + 0.561 \log \frac{N_t}{.584L_t}$$
$$(1.55) \qquad\qquad\qquad\qquad\qquad\qquad (2.57)$$

$$R^2 = .998 \ , \qquad D\text{-}W = 1.890$$

6. The Hours Worked Equation

$$\log h_t = -0.286 - 0.019 \log \frac{W_{t-1}}{P_{t-1}} + 0.246 \log h_{t-1} +$$
$$(2.8) \qquad (0.4) \qquad\qquad\qquad (7.1)$$

$$+ 0.216 \log CAP_t - 0.0995 \log \frac{Y_{t-1}}{L_t} -$$
$$(9.7) \qquad\qquad (2.4)$$

$$- 0.498 \ \log \frac{N_t}{.584L_t}$$
$$(5.8)$$

$$R^2 = .9807 \ , \qquad D\text{-}W = 1.293$$

The two identities are:

7. $Y_t = C_t + I_t + B_t$

8. $K_t = K_{t-1} + I_t$

The numbers in parentheses under the coefficients represent the t-statistics. The R^2 statistic is the usual measure of goodness of fit, and the Durbin-Watson (D-W) statistic is the measure of serial correlation in the residuals. The latter however is not a valid statistic when some of the regressors are lagged dependent variables. Because of low D-W values all the equations were reestimated by using the Cochrane and Orcutt Iterative Least Squares method for correction for autocorrelation. With the exception of the liquidity preference function, the coefficients in the other equations did not change very much. Therefore, we retained the liquidity preference function that was corrected for autocorrelation.

Before we consider the consumption function that was estimated simultaneously, we will discuss briefly the rest of the equations in the model.[15]

The liquidity preference function determines real cash holdings per dollar of income as a function of its lagged value, income, and the interest rate. All coefficients have the expected signs.

The production function is of the log-linear Cobb-Douglas type, with constant returns to scale. It determines output as a function of manhours of labor, adjusted for utilization via the employment ratio, and capital. A time trend accounts for technological change, which is estimated to add about 0.6 percent per year to output. The input coefficients imply elasticities of output with respect to labor of 0.751 and with respect to capital of 0.249.

The relative share equation is derived by equating the marginal product of labor to the real wage. According to this estimate, labor earns 75.1 percent of national income.

The fifth equation determines hourly earnings as a function of its lagged value, the current and lagged rate of price change, and the employment ratio, N/(.584)L; in the latter the expression (.584)L is an estimate of the civilian labor force.

The sixth equation determines hours worked as a function of its lagged value, the lagged real wage, the rate of capacity utilization, the income per capita, and the employment ratio.

Finally, equation 7 is the national income accounting identity, and equation 8 is the identity relating the change in capital stock to net investment.

Now we may return to the simultaneously estimated consumption function which is of great importance for our analysis. The first equation determines consumption per capita as a function of its lagged value, per capita income, real cash balances per capita, and government debt per capita.[16]   The last variable is the new element that we added to the Morishima-Saito framework. We introduced the debt per capita variable into the consumption function in order to analyze the impact of the pay-as-you-go OASI system on saving and capital formation. In other words, we assume that the operation of a pay-as-you-go pension system creates a type of public debt which is similar to the regular public debt which is issued by governments in order to finance government expenditures (these ideas were discussed more extensively in Chapter 9). This formulation of the problem will permit us to estimate the impact of the OASI program on saving in a general equilibrium framework, that is, as a solution to a system of simultaneous equations.

From the estimated consumption function we may estimate the following parameters, at the point of the sample means of the respective variables.

Marginal propensity to consume: $\dfrac{\partial(\frac{C}{L})}{\partial(\frac{Y}{L})} = 0.541$

The Pigou Effect : $\dfrac{\partial(\frac{C}{L})}{\partial(\frac{M}{PL})} = 0.404$

Marginal effect of lagged consumption: $\dfrac{\partial(\frac{C_t}{L_t})}{\partial(\frac{C_{t-1}}{L_{t-1}})} = 0.121$

The social security effect: $\dfrac{\partial(\frac{C}{L})}{\partial(\frac{D}{L})} = 0.172$

The above values are the short-run coefficients of the respective variables. We may derive "long-run" coefficients by using the Klein-Goldberger method, that is, by dividing each short-run coefficient by 1 minus the coefficient of the lagged consumption variable.[17]   Then, we will find that the long-run marginal propensity to consume is 0.615, and the long-run social security effect is 0.195.

It is observed that as soon as the rest of the domestic economy and the foreign sector (represented by the variable B) are taken into consideration the coefficient of the social security wealth variable

declines rapidly; that is, the present coefficient of
0.17 (or 0.19) is substantially lower than the estimated
coefficients derived from a separately estimated consumption function (the significant coefficients we derived
from Barro's specification of the consumption function
in the previous section were in the range 0.5 to 0.7).

We estimate that the reduction in the saving-
income ratio in 1972 was 14 percent (because (.172) X
(73.63) = 12.66 billions of 1972 dollars; also total
private saving in 1972 was 75.3 billion dollars). This
compares with our earlier estimated reduction of 26-33
percent (based on Barro's specification of the consumption function) and with Feldstein's estimate of 37
percent (however, he uses his own social security
wealth variable).

Moreover, our model permits us to estimate the
reduction in the saving-income ratio for the whole
period 1946-1978. During this period the mean value of
our social security wealth variable was 48.56 billions
in current dollars. This means that annual consumption
for this period was higher than it would have been in
the absence of the OASI program by $9.47 (= .195 X
48.56) billion on the average. The average total
private saving for the same period was $44.84 billion
annually. Hence, the reduction in saving due to the
operation of the OASI program was 17 percent on the
average for the period 1946-1978.

It would be interesting also to see how Feldstein's
social security wealth variable would fare in our
model.[18]   The following consumption function is
estimated simultaneously within the system of the
other equations of the model listed above.

We have:

$$\log \frac{C_t}{L_t} = -0.156 + 0.592 \log \frac{Y_t}{L_t} + 0.048 \log \frac{M_t}{L_t} +$$
$$\phantom{\log \frac{C_t}{L_t} = } (3.4) \qquad (14.0) \qquad\qquad (0.75)$$

$$+0.049 \log \frac{C_{t-1}}{L_{t-1}} + 0.150 \log \frac{D_t}{L_t}$$
$$ (2.7) \qquad\qquad (7.3)$$

Using the method employed above we may estimate
the "short-run" coefficient of the social security
variable; it is equal to 0.040 at the point of the
sample means of the respective variables. For year
1972, such a coefficient would imply a reduction in
the saving-income ratio of about 50 percent.

We ran also the same regression but instead of
using total government debt (the sum of regular public
debt and the social security wealth of Feldstein, as

above) we used in its place only Feldstein's social
security wealth variable. Then, the short-run coefficient was estimated at 0.05, which implies that in 1972
the saving-income ratio was reduced by more than 50
percent. Therefore, both estimates are much higher
than the 37 percent reduction that Feldstein estimated
when he used his single-equation consumption function.

ESTIMATES BASED ON A SIMULATION

In this section we will use a simulation to test
the theory developed in Chapter 11. One of the basic
conclusions of Chapter 11 was that the extra public
debt created by the operation of a pay-as-you-go
pension system reduces, across steady states, capital
intensiveness, output per capita, and consumption per
capita.

The macroeconomic model of long-run economic
growth for the American economy that was estimated in
the previous section will serve as the basis for a
historical simulation ("historical" means that the
simulation period coincides with the sample period)
that will determine the system's behavior under different assumptions concerning the amount of public debt
in the economy for the period 1946-1978. For this
period the amount of regular public debt per capita was
3.4348 thousands of 1972 dollars; when we add the
extra public debt created by the OASI program the
average total public debt per capita increases to
3.7477 thousands of 1972 dollars. Two simulations of
the long-run economic growth model will be made by
using the two values of public debt mentioned above.
The output of the simulations will be annual values of
capital, consumption, and income per capita under the
two alternative scenarios. Comparison of those values
will give us an estimate of the impact of the OASI
program on capital formation and economic growth.

From a technical point of view, the equations 1-8
of the previous section will have to be transformed
into the appropriate form. For that purpose we write:

$$y_t = \frac{Y_t}{L_t} \ , \ c_t = \frac{C_t}{L_t} \ , \ k_{t-1} = \frac{K_{t-1}}{L_t} \ , \ b_t = \frac{B_t}{L_t} \ , \ i_t = \frac{I_t}{L_t},$$

$$a_t = \frac{I_t}{Y_t} \ , \ d_t = \frac{D_t}{L_t}$$

Since we are interested in finding values for the
variables y_t, c_t, k_t, we will have to use only equa-

tions (1), (3), (4), (6), (7), and (8) of the whole
system of equations of the previous section. Actually
those six equations may determine: output per capita,
capital per capita, consumption per capita, investment
per capita, the real wage rate, and hours worked. This
means that certain variables will have to be kept
constant. Throughout the following analysis the following variables are fixed at the means of the respective
figures in the period 1946-1978:

$$\frac{N}{(.584)L} = .949 \ , \ \frac{M}{PY} = .513, \ \frac{B}{Y} = .009, \ CAP = 82.9$$

The constancy of the employment ratio, the
Cambridge coefficient, the ratio of trade balances, and
the ratio of capacity utilization are not realistic
assumptions, but they are necessary if we want to
reduce complexity in the model.

Now we are ready to transform equations (1), (3),
(4), (6), (7), (8). The relative share equation (4)
may be written as follows:

$$\log \frac{W_{t-1}}{P_{t-1}} = \log y_{t-1} + 0.132 \qquad (4')$$

If we substitute (4') into the hours worked equation
(6), we will obtain:

$$\log h_t = 0.1374 - 0.1185 \log y_{t-1} + 0.246 \log h_{t-1}$$

$$(6')$$

If we substitute (6') into the production function (3)
and simplify, we will obtain:

$$\log y_t = 1.053 - 0.089 \log y_{t-1} + 0.184 \log h_{t-1}$$

$$+ 0.249 \log k_{t-1} + 0.00625t \qquad (3')$$

In the production function we used k_{t-1} instead of k_t,
and also we set the dummy variable U^{t-1} equal to 1.

If we substitute (3') into the consumption function (1) and simplify, we will obtain:

$$\log c_t = -0.033 - 0.098 \log y_{t-1} + 0.202 \log h_{t-1} +$$

$$+ 0.007t + 0.273 \log k_{t-1} + 0.116 \log c_{t-1} +$$

$$+ 0.158 \ \log d \qquad (1')$$

Also, we have by definition:

$$i_t = a_t \, y_t \qquad \text{and} \qquad b_t = 0.009 \, y_t$$

Then, the national income accounting identity (7) may be written as follows:

$$\log \frac{c_t}{y_t} = \log (1 - a_t - 0.009)$$

If we substitute (1') and (3') in the expression above and simplify, we will obtain:

$$\log (1 - a_t - 0.009) = -0.543 - 0.009 \log y_{t-1} + 0.00075t$$
$$0.018 \log h_{t-1} + 0.024 \log k_{t-1} +$$
$$+ 0.116 \log c_{t-1} + 0.158 \log d \qquad (7')$$

Finally, from identity (8) of the previous section we derive that:

$$K_t = (1 + g_t) \, K_{t-1} \quad \text{and} \quad g_t \, K_{t-1} = I_t$$

where g_t is the rate of capital accumulation in period t. Dividing both of the above equations by $L_{t+1} = n \cdot L_t$ (where n = 1.01378, which is the average rate of growth of the population aged sixteen years and over for the period 1946-1978) we obtain:

$$1.01378 \, k_t = (1 + g_t) \, k_{t-1} \qquad \text{(i)}$$

and

$$g_t \, k_{t-1} = a_t \cdot y_t \qquad \text{(ii)}$$

If we substitute (ii) in (i) we obtain:

$$k_t = \frac{1}{1.01378} (k_{t-1} + a_t \cdot y_t)$$
$$\qquad (8')$$

or

$$\log k_t = \log (k_{t-1} + a_t \, y_t) - 0.0059$$

The system of equations (6'), (3'), (1'), (7'), and (8') determines h_t, y_t, c_t, a_t and k_t respectively when h_{t-1}, y_{t-1}, c_{t-1}, a_{t-1}, k_{t-1} are given. The simulation starts with the actual values of the respective variables in 1946.[19] We ran two simulations: the first was based on the assumption that the U.S. OASI program creates annually a certain amount of public debt that has the same impact on the economy as

the regular public debt; the second simulation is
based on the assumption that the OASI program does not
create any type of public debt. In the former case
the value of d (= D/L) is set equal to its actual
value for the period 1946-1978 which is 3.7477 thousands of 1972 dollars; the simulated values of k_t, y_t,
and c_t are shown in Table 12.4 (for k_t) and Tables
E.1 and E.2 (for y_t, c_t) of Appendix E.
    In the case where we assume that the OASI program
does not affect the economy, the value of d (= D/L) is
set equal to its actual value for the period 1946-1978
which is 3.4348 thousands of 1972 dollars (that is,
this figure refers only to the regular interest-bearing
public debt per capita); the simulated values of k_t
are shown in Table 12.4, and the simulated values of y_t
and c_t are shown in Tables E.1 and E.2 of Appendix E.
    From Table 12.4 we see that on the average for
the period 1946-1978 the capital-labor ratio for the
American economy would have been 10.1540; however the
presence of the OASI program has reduced the capital-
labor ratio to 9.2475. Hence, the social security
program has resulted in an 8.9 percent reduction of
the capital-labor ratio on the average over the period
from 1946 to 1978.
    Using the production function that was estimated
earlier and which has an elasticity of production with
respect to capital equal to 0.25, we may find that the
8.9 percent reduction in capital has reduced output by
2.22 percent. Indeed, this result is also confirmed
from the information in Table E.1 (in Appendix E);
there we see that in the absence of the OASI program
output per capita would have been equal to 7.1052 on
the average for the period 1946-1978, however, the
presence of the pension system resulted in an output-
labor ratio of 6.9555. That is, the operation of the
OASI program resulted in a decrease of 2.1 percent in
output per capita. The consequent reduction in consumption per capita over the period 1946-1978 is
similarly estimated (from the average values given in
Table E.2 in Appendix E) to be about 0.9 percent on
the average.
    Finally, we should mention that the whole simula-
tion was run again by using Feldstein's social security
wealth variable instead of our own. The value of d (=
D/L) for the simulation was 13.0982 thousands of 1972
dollars. The simulation showed that if Feldstein's
d = 13.0982 were operative in the American economy
during the period 1946-1978 the capital-labor ratio
would, on the average, tend to decline continuously
and almost disappear in the late 1970's.

TABLE 12.4
Actual and Predicted Capital-Labor Ratios
(in Thousands of 1972 Dollars)

Year	Actual $\frac{K}{L}$	Predicted K/L When d = 3.7477	Predicted K/L When d = 3.4348
1946	6.081	6.081	6.081
1947	6.428	6.285	6.285
1948	6.759	6.633	6.685
1949	6.974	6.965	7.077
1950	7.290	7.278	7.450
1951	7.967	7.570	7.802
1952	7.762	7.842	8.134
1953	7.943	8.094	8.446
1954	8.164	8.326	8.737
1955	8.452	8.538	9.008
1956	8.724	8.730	9.258
1957	8.948	8.902	9.488
1958	9.100	9.054	9.696
1959	9.308	9.186	9.884
1960	9.467	9.299	10.052
1961	9.634	9.391	10.199
1962	9.839	9.464	10.325
1963	10.028	9.518	10.431
1964	10.265	9.682	10.673
1965	10.582	9.909	10.975
1966	10.904	10.164	11.301
1967	11.142	10.399	11.608
1968	11.402	10.604	11.882
1969	11.675	10.776	12.122
1970	11.840	10.915	12.327
1971	12.035	11.025	12.509
1972	12.240	11.011	12.564
1973	12.538	10.940	12.558
1974	12.678	10.834	12.514
1975	12.638	10.700	12.437
1976	12.771	10.539	12.330
1977	13.001	10.353	12.194
1978	13.327	10.143	12.029

Mean Value: 9.9362   9.2475   10.1540

150

CONCLUSIONS

The evidence presented in this chapter suggests
that Professor Feldstein was correct in his qualitative conclusion concerning the adverse effect of the
pay-as-you-go pension system on capital formation, but
it seems that he has overestimated the size of this
effect.

Our evidence, when based on single-equation
consumption function estimates, gives mixed results.
Based on specifications of the consumption function
similar to those of Feldstein and Darby, we find no
significant adverse effect, in either an economic or
statistical sense, of the U.S. OASI program on capital
formation. On the other hand, when we use Barro's
specification of the consumption function we find
that the OASI program has reduced the saving-income
ratio by about 26 to 33 percent. We may conclude then
that our results are sensitive to the specification of
the consumption function.

When we estimate the consumption function simultaneously, that is, within the context of a long-run
model of the U.S. economy, we find that the reduction
in the saving-income ratio due to the operation of the
OASI program is on the average about 14 to 17 percent.
Moreover, it should be noted that the use of Feldstein's concept of social security wealth in the same
type of analysis results in an estimated reduction of
the saving-income ratio of more than 50 percent.

Finally, a simulation of the American economy for
the period 1946-1978 shows that the increased amount
of public debt per capita, caused by the operation of
the OASI program, has resulted in a decrease of 8.9
percent in the amount of capital that would be available in the absence of the public pension program.
The use of Feldstein's concept of social security
wealth in the same type of simulation results in an
estimated reduction in capital formation of more than
80 percent.

Table 12.5 summarizes the evidence found in this
chapter and compares it to the results found by
Feldstein, Barro, and Darby. The second column shows
the estimated reduction in capital formation when the
analysis is based on Feldstein's social security
wealth variable. The third and fourth columns present
the estimated reduction in capital formation when use
is made of the new social security wealth variable
that we constructed in Chapter 9.

Taken as a whole, our evidence suggests that the
operation of the U.S. OASI program has reduced capital
formation by about 10 to 15 percent. In a climate of

TABLE 12.5
Estimated Percentage Reduction in Capital Formation
because of Social Security

Type of Specification	Feldstein's SSW variable; Estimates for 1971-1972	New SSW variable; Estimates for	
		1972	1946-1978
Feldstein	$37^{(2)}$	0	---
Barro	$0^{(2)}$	26-33	---
Darby	29 and $-42.6^{(1)\,(2)}$	0	---
Simultaneous System	50	14	17
Simulation	80	12	8.9

(1) The first estimate is derived when the M2 defini-
    tion of money supply applies to the money concept
    included in the regression. When the M1 definition
    is used, it is estimated that social security
    increases capital formation.

(2) These estimates were taken from the sources
    mentioned in Note 2.   All the other estimates
    shown on Table 12.5 were derived in this chapter.

anxiety over a capital shortage, such an estimate
raises some concern about the economic impact of social
security. This concern has been expressed in several
proposals, including one to change social security from
a pay-as-you-go basis to a fully funded basis. We dis-
posed of the latter argument in Chapter 10 and we will
not reconsider it here. However, we would like to
mention two factors that reduce the importance of the
finding of an adverse effect of the social security
system on capital formation.

The first factor is the proven capacity of pay-as-
you-go pension systems to satisfy all the basic objectives of dynamic pensions. The adverse effect of the
system on capital formation should be weighed against
this relative advantage of the system.

A second factor that reduces the importance of our
finding is the expansion of private pension plans.
Coverage under these plans has increased rapidly over
the last three decades. To the extent that such
pension plans are underfunded, they have probably
reduced saving, so that our estimate of a modest
reduction in saving, due to social security, may actually be an overestimate; in other words, our social
security wealth variable may be picking up the consumption effect of growing private wealth.

Moreover, as the OASI program matures, the rate of
return on contributions will become equal to or less
than the growth rate of the economy; this might induce
additional saving that will make up the past capital
deficiency.

NOTES

1. The construction of this variable is described in Chapter 9.

2. See Martin Feldstein, "Social Security, Induced Retirement and Aggregate Capital Accumulation." Journal of Political Economy, Vol. 82, Sept./Oct. 1974, pp. 905-926; Robert Barro, The Impact of Social Security on Private Saving: Evidence from the U.S. Time Series (Washington D.C.: American Enterprise Institute, 1978); Michael Darby, The Effects of Social Security on Income and the Capital Stock (Washington, D.C.: American Enterprise Institute, 1979).

3. See Albert Ando and Franco Modigliani, "The Life Cycle Hypothesis of Saving: Aggregate Implications and Tests", American Economic Review, Vol. 53, March 1963, pp. 55-84.

4. Data on C_t, Y_t, RE_t and U_t are taken from the Economic Report of the President (Washington D.C.: Government Printing Office, 1980). Nominal values are deflated by the deflator for personal consumption expenditure (1972 = 100). Population is total, including armed forces overseas. Data on the deflator and population are taken also from the Economic Report of the President (1980). The wealth variable, W_t, is reported in Martin Feldstein, Government Deficits and Aggregate Demand, National Bureau of Economic Research, Working Paper No. 435, January 1980, p. 36. Finally, the SSW_t variable is taken from Table 9.4 of Chapter 9, for m = 35 years, where m is average length of working life.

5. This transformation was suggested by Barro in "The Impact of Social Security..." and Feldstein used it in his most recent reestimation of the extended consumption function; see Martin Feldstein, "Comment", Social Security Bulletin, Vol. 42, No. 5, May 1979, pp. 36-50.

6. The consumer expenditure function was developed by Darby. See M.R. Darby, "The Consumer Expenditure Function", Explorations in Economic Research, Vol. 4, Winter/Spring 1977-1978, pp. 645-674.

7. Data on all variables except the SSW variable are taken from Robert Barro: The Impact of Social Security on Private Saving: Evidence from the U.S. Time Series, Ibid., pp. 10-14. The SSW variable was constructed on the basis of the method developed in Chapter 9 for m = 35 years of working life; the current dollar estimates were transformed into 1958 dollars by using the deflator for personal consumption expenditures (1958 = 100). The annual values of the SSW variable in 1958 dollars are shown in Appendix C.

The population variable is total population, including armed forces overseas; it is taken from the same source as in Note 4 above.

8. See discussion in R. Barro: The Impact of Social Security..., Ibid, pp. 5-16.

9. Ibid, pp. 17-18 and p. 21.

10. See "Reply" by M. Feldstein in R. Barro: The Impact of Social Security..., Ibid, pp. 37-47.

11. The estimated reductions in the saving-income ratio are calculated as follows: the coefficient of the SSW variable is applied to the respective year's social security wealth: the amount found is considered as the extra would-be saving and it is added to this year's total private savings (= total personal saving + undistributed corporate profits). The ratio of those two magnitudes serves as the estimate of the reduction in the saving-income ratio. Feldstein in his original 1974 article considered also the amount of the collected annual social security taxes as extra (and therefore lost) savings; later however he abandoned this calculation method (see his "comment" in Social Security Bulletin, Vol. 42, May 1979, p. 38), presumably because he recognized that social security taxes are automatically transformed into social security benefits and therefore disposable income or savings is not affected at all.

12. Data on all variables except the SSW variable are taken from Michael Darby: The Effects of Social Security on Income and the Capital Stock, Ibid, pp. 54-63. Darby used in his regressions both the M1 and M2 concepts of money supply; we used only the M1. As far as the SSW variable is concerned, its construction and annual values are given in Appendix C.

13. See M. Morishima and M. Saito, "A Dynamic Analysis of the American Economy, 1902-1952", in M. Morishima et al., The Workings of Econometric Models (New York: Cambridge University Press, 1972), pp. 3-69.

14. The instrumental variables used in the estimation of our system are: $\log (C_{t-1}/L_{t-1})$, $\log M_{t-1}$, $\log (W_{t-1}/h_{t-1})$, $\log (P_{t-1}/P_{t-2})$, $\log (W_{t-1} \cdot P_{t-1} \cdot h_{t-1})$, $\log (I_t + B_t)$, $\log (D_t/L_t)$, $\log L_t$, $\log (M_t/L_t)$, $\log (N_t/.584 L_t)$, t, u.

15. For a discussion of the rationale of the equations of the model see Morishima and Saito, "A Dynamic Analysis..." Ibid, pp. 7-24. With the exception of the consumption function our specified equations follow closely the original Morishima-Saito specifications.

16. We reestimated the consumption function by using a wealth variable, W, (for its source see Note 4

above) in the place of the cash balances variables. As
the following estimated function shows,the coefficients
of most variables are altered, but, and this is important for our purposes, the coefficient of debt per
capita did not change substantially. It is:

$$\log \frac{C_t}{L_t} = -0.410 + 0.566 \log \frac{Y_t}{L_t} \pm 0.015 \log \frac{C_{t-1}}{L_{t-1}} +$$
$$\quad\quad\quad (2.75) \quad (7.0) \quad\quad\quad (.64)$$

$$+ 0.212 \log \frac{W_t}{L_t} + 0.149 \log \frac{D_t}{L_t}$$
$$\quad (6.61) \quad\quad\quad (2.50)$$

17. The Klein-Goldberger method is mentioned in
Morishima and Saito, "A Dynamic Analysis...", Ibid,
pp. 8-9.
18. Feldstein's social security wealth variable,
expressed in 1972 dollars, is given in Martin
Feldstein, Government Deficits and Aggregate Demand,
National Bureau of Economic Research, Working paper No.
435, January 1980, p. 36.
19. In order to improve the ability of the model
to "track", we changed the constant terms of equations
(6'), (3'), and (1') to the following terms respectively: 0.3100, 0.528, and 0.216 for the period 1946-
1962. The corresponding values for the period 1963-
1969 were: 0.1374, 0.528, and 0.216. Finally, the
constant terms for the period 1970-1978 were set equal
to 0.3100, 0.7100, and 0.196 respectively. In choosing
the values of the constant terms, the criterion was
always to improve the ability of the model to track
the actual capital-labor ratios.

Part 4

Appendices

Appendix A:
A Demographic Model

In this appendix we will state more explicitly the demographic background of the model used in the main text of Chapter 6.

The population we have in mind was Lo in time zero (for convenience Lo may be set equal to 1 in calculations). We are interested in the composition of this population after t years. Our main concern is with the portion of the total population which is in the labor force, and also the portion which is in retirement. The growth rate of the population is n annually, and the birth rate is d annually.

As far as the working population is concerned, people enter the labor force at the age of 16 and retire upon attainment of age 65. The age distribution of workers at year t is:

Group of workers of age 16: $d \cdot Lo \cdot e^{n(t-16)}$

Group of workers of age 17: $d \cdot Lo \cdot e^{n(t-17)}$

$$\begin{matrix} \cdot & & \cdot \\ \cdot & & \cdot \\ \cdot & & \cdot \\ \cdot & & \cdot \end{matrix}$$

Group of workers of age 64: $d \cdot Lo \cdot e^{n(t-64)}$

Generally,

Group of workers of age (16+k): $d \cdot Lo \cdot e^{n(t-k)}$

or

$$d \cdot L \cdot e^{n(t-64)} \cdot e^{n(64-k)}, \ \forall \ k = 0, 1, 2, \ldots 48$$

The total labor force at year t, L_t, may be obtained by summing up the members of each age group for all ages between 16 and 65.
We have :

$$L_t = d \cdot Lo \cdot e^{n(t-16)} + d \cdot Lo \cdot e^{n(t-17)} + \ldots +$$

$$+ d \cdot Lo \cdot e^{n(t-64)}$$

$$= d \cdot Lo \cdot e^{n(t-64)} \ (e^{48n} + e^{47n} + \ldots + e^{n} + 1)$$

$$= d \cdot Lo \cdot e^{n(t-64)} \cdot \int_{0}^{48} e^{nt} \, dt$$

or

$$L_t = d \cdot Lo \cdot \frac{1}{n} \cdot e^{n(t-64)} \cdot (e^{48n} - 1)$$

The ratio of the age group $(16+k)$, $k = 0, 1, 2, \ldots$ 48, to the total labor force, L_t, denoted by f_k, is given by the general relationship:

$$f_k = \frac{d \cdot Lo \cdot n \cdot e^{n(t-64)} \cdot e^{n(64-k)}}{d \cdot Lo \cdot e^{n(t-64)} \ (e^{48n} - 1)} \implies f_k = \frac{n \cdot e^{n(64-k)}}{e^{48n} - 1}$$

and therefore:

$$f_{(16+k)} = \frac{n \cdot e^{n(48-k)}}{e^{48n} - 1} \ , \quad \forall \ k = 0, 1, 2, \ldots, 48.$$

As far as the retired population is concerned, we assume that retirement life starts at the beginning of the year in which workers reach age 65. Retired people die at the rate δ percent annually; deaths are concentrated at the beginning of the year.
The age distribution of the retired population is:

Group of retired of age 65: $d \cdot Lo \cdot e^{-\delta} \cdot e^{n(t-65)}$

Group of retired of age 66: $d \cdot Lo \cdot e^{-2\delta} \cdot e^{n(t-66)}$

$$\vdots \qquad\qquad\qquad \vdots$$

Generally,

Group of retired of age $(65 + \mu)$: $d \cdot Lo \cdot e^{-(\mu+1)\delta} \cdot$
$$\cdot e^{n(t-65-\mu)}$$

or

$$d \cdot Lo \cdot e^{-(\mu+1)\delta} \cdot e^{n(t-64)} \cdot e^{-n\mu}, \ \forall \ \mu = 0, 1, 2, \ldots \infty.$$

We may obtain the total retired population at year t, R_t, by summing up the members of each age group for all ages between 65 and $+\infty$.
We have:

$$R_t = d \cdot Lo \cdot (e^{-\delta} \cdot e^{n(t-65)} + e^{-2\delta} \cdot e^{n(t-66)} + \ldots)$$

$$= d \cdot Lo \cdot e^{-\delta} \cdot e^{n(t-65)} \cdot (1 + e^{-\delta} \cdot e^{-n} + e^{-2\delta} \cdot e^{-2n} + \ldots)$$

$$= d \cdot Lo \cdot e^{-\delta} \cdot e^{n(t-65)} \cdot \int_0^{+\infty} e^{-(\delta+n)t} \, dt =$$

$$= d \cdot Lo \cdot e^{-\delta} \cdot e^{n(t-65)} \cdot \frac{-1}{\delta+n} \, (-1)$$

because: if $\lambda < 0$, then $e^{\lambda t} \rightarrow 0$ as $t \rightarrow +\infty$

Hence:

$$R_t = d \cdot Lo \cdot \frac{1}{\delta+n} \, e^{-\delta} \cdot e^{n(t-65)}$$

Finally, the ratio of the age group $(65 + n)$ to the total retired population, denoted by g_μ, $\mu = 0, 1, 2, \ldots +\infty$, is given by the general relationship:

$$g_{(65+\mu)} = \frac{d \cdot Lo \cdot e^{-(\mu+1)\delta} \cdot e^{n(t-65)} \cdot e^{-n\mu}}{d \cdot Lo \cdot \frac{1}{\delta+n} \cdot e^{-\delta} \cdot e^{n(t-65)}}$$

or

$$g_{(65+\mu)} = (\delta + n) \cdot e^{-\mu(\delta+n)}, \forall \mu = 0, 1, 2, \ldots +\infty$$

Appendix B:
Description and Sources
of Variables used in Chapter 7

Only variables γ, B, E and Λ require some additional explanation.

The replacement rate, γ, for the "average" retiree is calculated as the ratio of the average annual pension to the average annual earnings of the current "average" worker. The simulations shown in Columns (8), (11), and (12) of Table 7.1 (of Chapter 7) are based on a replacement rate, γ, which is calculated in relation to the annual average "taxable" earnings (that is, earnings taxed by the payroll tax); whereas Column (13) refers to a simulation in which γ is expressed in terms of annual average total earnings. Both types of earnings are reported in the <u>Annual Statistical Supplement of the Social Security Bulletin</u> (Washington, D.C.: U.S. Dept. of H.E.W., Social Security Administration, 1976), p. 76. Furthermore, the average annual pension is calculated as the average monthly pension for the "average retiree" times 12 months; the average monthly pension is calculated as the weighted average of the average monthly pension of the group "retired workers" and that of the group "dependents and survivors". For those two groups, data about their numbers are given in the <u>Annual Statistical Supplement</u> (1975), Table 55, page 88, and <u>Social Security Bulletin</u>, Vol. 42, No. 12, December 1979, Table M-10, page 31. Also, the respective average pensions for those two groups are given in the <u>Annual Statistical Supplement</u> (1976), Table 82, page 132, and <u>Social Security Bulletin</u>, Vol. 42, No. 12, December 1979, Table M-13, page 34.

As far as the B variable is concerned (that is, the degree of coverage of the civilian labor force by the OASI program), its annual values have increased from 59 percent in 1950 to 86 percent in 1978. The civilian labor force is roughly equal to the sum of paid civilian employment plus unpaid family workers plus the unemployed plus the Armed Forces; the second group is probably the one that has not yet been

163

covered adequately by the OASI program. Data for
pension coverage are given in the Annual Statistical
Supplement (1976), Table 7, p. 48, and U.S. Bureau of
the Census, Statistical Abstract of the United States
(Washington, D.C.: Government Printing Office, 1979),
p. 331.

The category "newly retired" is equivalent to the
category "total awards" (includes awards currently
payable and conditional or deferred awards) in the
Annual Statistical Supplement; data for years 1950-
1959 are given in the 1960 issue, Table 29, page 26,
and Table 42, page 31; data for years 1960-1978 are
from the 1976 issue, Table 58, page 99, and Social
Security Bulletin, Vol. 42, No. 12, December 1979,
Table M-16, page 37.

Finally, the already retired are obtained by subtracting the "newly retired" from the "total retired";
the latter group is the sum of "retired workers" and
"dependents and survivors" (see above).

The actual payroll tax, ACT, in Table 7.1 of
Chapter 7 is the total tax for the employer and the
employee. Data for the OASI program are taken from
Alicia H. Munnell, The Future of Social Security
(Washington, D.C.: Brookings Institution, 1977), Table
A-12, pages 182-183.

Finally, data for the unemployment rate and the
growth rate of productivity are taken from the
Economic Report of the President (Washington, D.C.:
Government Printing Office, 1979).

Appendix C:
Social Security Wealth in 1958 Dollars

The social security wealth variable is normally constructed by using equation (3) in Chapter 9. The value of m (= length of working life) is set equal to 35 years. The estimated annual values of the SSW variable are deflated by using the deflator for personal consumption expenditure (1958 = 100). The values for the period 1950-1974 are shown below.

TABLE C.1
Estimated Annual Values of Social Security Wealth
(Billions of 1958 dollars)

Year	SSW	Year	SSW
1946		1960	21.4040
1947		1961	21.0879
1948		1962	23.2944
1949		1963	27.7820
1950	6.0768	1964	29.0359
1951	7.9868	1965	30.7297
1952	9.0819	1966	38.3307
1953	8.9377	1967	39.1907
1954	11.0224	1968	40.6135
1955	13.6324	1969	46.5642
1956	14.4946	1970	43.8709
1957	14.3655	1971	47.7029
1958	13.5763	1972	53.2813
1959	17.4644	1973	63.4284
		1974	63.6899

Appendix D:
Names and Sources of Variables used in the Simultaneous Equation System

The variables C (= consumption), N(= persons engaged in employment), B (= trade balance), L (= population sixteen years of age and over), and CAP(= capacity utilization rate in manufacturing, F.R.B. Series) are taken from the Economic Report of the President (Washington, D.C.: Government Printing Office, 1980).

Variable Y (= net national product in 1972 billions of dollars) is taken from the Survey of Current Business, Vol. 56, No. 1, Part II, January 1976, Page 16; and later issues. Net National Product at current dollars is taken from the Economic Report of the President (1980), Ibid. The ratio of the later divided by the former gives the price variable, P, the base of which is 1972 = 1.

The capital variable, K, is the total sum of net stocks of fixed nonresidential business capital and net stocks of residential capital. Values for the period 1946-1975 are given (in 1972 dollars) in the Survey of Current Business, Vol. 56, No. 4, April 1976, pp. 46-52; Table 4, column 1, and Table 8, column 1. Values of K for the years 1976, 1977, and 1978 were found as follows: we deflated the annual net investment for those years by the deflator of personal consumption expenditure (1972 = 100); the result for each year was added to the already existing stock of capital.

The annual money wage, W, and the annual hours worked, h, were found by multiplying the weekly magnitudes of the respective variables by 50. The weekly magnitudes are given in the Economic Report of the President (1980), Ibid.

The corporate bond yield, r, is the Moody's Aaa measure of corporate bond yield. It is expressed in percentage terms per annum. Data are from the Economic Report of the President (1980), Ibid, page 278.

The annual net investment, I, was found by
deflating current dollar estimates by the deflator for
personal consumption expenditure (1972 = 100). The
deflator is given in the Economic Report of the
President (1980), Ibid.

The cash balances variable, M, stands for the M2
version of money supply. It is taken from the
Economic Report of the President, Ibid, various
issues.

Total government debt, D, is the total sum of
the annual interest-bearing public debt securities
and the annual amount of debt created by the OASI
program. The latter is given in Table 9.4 of Chapter
9 (in 1972 dollars). The former is transformed into
1972 dollars by using the deflator for personal
consumption expenditure (1972 = 100).

Appendix E:
Actual and Simulated Values

This Appendix includes:

168

TABLE E.1
Actual and Predicted Output-Labor Ratios
(in Thousands of 1972 Dollars)

Year	Actual $\frac{Y}{L}$	Predicted Y/L When d = 3.7477	Predicted Y/L When d = 3.4348
1946	4.329	4.329	4.329
1947	4.178	4.258	4.258
1948	4.294	4.367	4.367
1949	4.255	4.483	4.491
1950	4.595	4.591	4.608
1951	4.925	4.695	4.721
1952	5.057	4.797	4.831
1953	5.164	4.897	4.938
1954	5.025	4.995	5.043
1955	5.322	5.091	5.147
1956	5.375	5.186	5.249
1957	5.402	5.278	5.349
1958	5.314	5.369	5.447
1959	5.581	5.459	5.544
1960	5.613	5.547	5.639
1961	5.681	5.634	5.733
1962	5.945	5.719	5.826
1963	6.077	5.803	5.917
1964	6.301	6.318	8.490
1965	6.578	8.058	8.236
1966	6.868	8.144	8.332
1967	6.927	8.287	8.486
1968	7.104	8.435	8.645
1969	7.154	8.581	8.802
1970	6.974	8.722	8.954
1971	7.054	9.531	9.794
1972	7.309	9.787	10.068
1973	7.569	9.926	10.224
1974	7.249	10.042	10.356
1975	7.035	10.149	10.482
1976	7.358	10.251	10.602
1977	7.590	10.348	10.718
1978	7.782	10.440	10.829

Mean Value : 6.0304   6.9555   7.1052

TABLE E.2
Actual and Predicted Consumption-Labor Ratios
(in Thousands of 1972 Dollars)

Year	Actual $\frac{C}{L}$	Predicted C/L When d = 3.7477	Predicted C/L When d = 3.4348
1946	2.939	2.939	2.939
1947	2.961	2.960	2.960
1948	2.993	3.032	2.991
1949	3.030	3.130	3.089
1950	3.171	3.226	3.190
1951	3.178	3.319	3.289
1952	3.225	3.411	3.386
1953	3.292	3.501	3.482
1954	3.323	3.590	3.576
1955	3.505	3.677	3.669
1956	3.570	3.764	3.761
1957	3.602	3.849	3.852
1958	3.599	3.934	3.942
1959	3.744	4.017	4.031
1960	3.781	4.100	4.119
1961	3.810	4.181	4.206
1962	3.926	4.261	4.292
1963	4.006	4.341	4.378
1964	4.156	4.078	4.118
1965	4.319	3.911	3.956
1966	4.467	3.939	3.989
1967	4.525	4.020	4.075
1968	4.671	4.110	4.171
1969	4.756	4.200	4.267
1970	4.771	4.095	4.165
1971	4.852	4.502	4.584
1972	5.027	4.643	4.734
1973	5.176	4.784	4.884
1974	5.041	4.858	4.968
1975	5.046	4.925	5.046
1976	5.256	4.989	5.120
1977	5.433	5.050	5.192
1978	5.591	5.108	5.261
Mean Value:	4.0835	4.0139	4.0514

Bibliography

Aaron, Henry. "The Social Insurance Paradox."
Canadian Journal of Economics and Political
Science. Vol. 32 (August 1966), pp. 371-374.
_____. "Demographic Effects on the Equity of
Social Security Benefits." in the Economics of
Public Services. Edited by M. Feldstein and R.
Inman. International Economic Association
Series, 1977.
Ando, Albert and Modigliani, Franco. "The Life Cycle
Hypothesis of Saving: Aggregate Implications
and Tests" American Economic Review. Vol. 53
(March 1963), pp. 54-84.
Arrow, Kenneth. "Uncertainty and the Welfare Economics
of Medical Care." American Economic Review, Vol.
53 (December 1963), pp. 941-973.
_____. "The Role of Securities in the Optimal
Allocation of Risk-bearing." Review of Economic
Studies . Vol. 31 (April 1964), pp. 91-96.
_____. "Limited knowledge and Economic Analysis."
American Economic Review, Vol. 64 (March 1974),
pp. 1-10.
Arrow, Kenneth and Lind, R.C. "Uncertainty and the
Evaluation of Public Investment Decisions."
American Economic Review. Vol. 60 (June 1970),
pp. 364-378.
Arthur, Brian, W. and McNicoll, Geoffrey. "Samuelson,
Population, and Intergenerational Transfers."
International Economic Review. Vol. 19 (February
1978), pp. 241-246.
Asimakopoulos, A. "The Biological Interest Rate and
the Social Utility Function." American Economic
Review, Vol. 57 (March 1967), pp. 185-190.
_____. The Nature of Public Pension Plans: Inter-
generational Equity, Funding, and Saving.
Economic Council of Canada. Hull, Quebec, Canada:
Canadian Government Publishing Center, 1980.
Asimakopoulos, A. and Weldon, J.C. "On the Theory of
Government Pension Plan." Canadian Journal of
Economics, Vol. 1 (November 1968), pp. 699-717.
_____. "On Private Plans in the Theory of Pensi-
ons." Canadian Journal of Economics, Vol. 3
(May 1970), pp. 223-237.
Atkinson, A.B. "National Superannuation: Redistribu-
tion and Value for Money." Bulletin of the
Oxford University Institute of Economics and
Statistics. Vol. 32 (August 1970), pp. 171-185.
Bailey, Martin. National Income and the Price Level.
New York: McGraw-Hill Book Co., 1971.
Bankers Trust Company. A Study of Industrial Retire-
ment Plans. New York: Bankers Trust Co., 1975.

Barro, Robert. "Are Government Bonds Net Wealth."
Journal of Political Economy, Vol. 82 (July/
August 1974), pp. 1095-1117.
_____. "Reply to Feldstein and Buchanan." Journal
of Political Economy, Vol. 84 (April 1976), pp.
343-349.
_____. The Impact of Social Security on Private
Saving: Evidence from U.S. Time Series. Washing-
gton D.C.: American Enterprise Institute, 1978.
Barro, Robert, and MacDonald, G.M. "Social Security
and Consumer Spending in an International Cross
Section." Journal of Public Economics. Vol. 11
(June 1979), pp. 275-289.
Blackburn, John. "The Social Insurance Paradox: A
Comment." Canadian Journal of Economics and
Political Science. Vol. 33 (1967), pp. 445-446.
Boskin, Michael. "Social Security and Retirement
Decisions." Economic Inquiry, Vol. 15 (January
1977), pp. 1-25.
Boskin, M. and Hurd, M. "The Effect of Social Secu-
rity on Early Retirement." Journal of Public
Economics, Vol. 10 (1978), pp. 361-377.
Bowen, W.G., Davis, R.G., Kopf, D.H. "The Public
Debt: A Burden on Future Generaltions."
American Economic Review, Vol. 50 (1960), pp.
701-706.
Boyle, P. and Murray, J. "Social Security Wealth and
Private Saving in Canada." Canadian Journal of
Economics. Vol. 12 (August 1979), pp. 456-468.
Brainard, W. and Dolbear, F.T. "Social Risk and
Financial Markets." American Economic Review
(Papers and Proceedings). Vol. 61 (May 1971),
pp. 360-370.
Break, George. "The Economic Effects of Social Secu-
rity's OASI Program." University of California,
Berkeley, March 1980. Mimeograph.
Brittain, John. "The Real Rate of Interest on Life-
time Contributions Toward Retirement under Social
Security." in Old Age Income Assurance, Part III:
Public Programs, Joint Economic Committee, 90th
Congress, 1st Session. Washington, D.C.: Govern-
ment Printing Office, 1976.
Browning, Edgar K. "Social Insurance and Intergenera-
tional Transfers." Journal of Law and Economics.
Vol. 16 (October 1973), pp. 215-237.
Buchanan, James M. "Social Insurance in a Growing
Economy: A Proposal for Radical Reform."
National Tax Journal. Vol. 21 (October 1968),
pp. 376-394.
Buiter, Willem. "Crowding Out and the Effectiveness
of Fiscal Policy." Journal of Public Economics.
Vol. 7 (1977), pp. 309-328.

Cagan, Philip. The Effect of Pension Plans on Aggre-
gate Savings, National Bureau of Economic
Research, 1965.
Campbell, C.D. "Social Insurance in the United States:
A Program in Search of an Explanation," Journal
of Law and Economics. Vol. 12 (October 1969),
pp. 249-266.
_____ . Editor, Income Redistribution, Washington
D.C.: American Enterprise Institute, 1977.
Campbell, C.D. and Campbell, R.G. "Cost Benefit
Ratios under the Federal Old-Age Insurance
Program." in Old Age Income Assurance, Part III:
Public Programs, Joint Economic Committee, 90th
Congress, 1st Session. Washington, D.C.: Govern-
ment Printing Office, 1967.
_____ . "Conflicting Views on the Effect of Old-
Age and Survivors Insurance on Retirement."
Economic Inquiry, Vol. 14 (September 1976), pp.
369-388.
Cass, David and Yaari, Menahem. "A Re-examination of
the Pure Consumption Loans Model." Journal of
Political Economy. Vol. 74 (1966), pp. 353-367.
Chen, Y.-P. and Chu, K.W. "Tax Benefit Ratios and
Rates of Return under OASI: 1974 Retirees and
Entrants." Journal of Risk and Insurance, Vol.
41 (June 1974), pp. 189-206.
Clark, R.L. "Increasing Income Transfers to the Elder-
ly Implied by Zero Population Growth." Review of
Social Economy, Vol. 35 (April 1977), pp. 37-54.
Darby, Michael. "The Consumer Expenditure Function."
Explorations in Economic Research. Vol. 4
(Winter-Spring 1977-1978), pp. 645-674.
_____ . The Effects of Social Security on Income
and the Capital Stock. Washington, D.C.:
American Enterprise Institute, 1979.
David, P.A. and Scadding, J.L. "Private Savings:
Ultrarationality, Aggregation, and Denison's Law."
Journal of Political Economy. Vol. 82 (March/
April 1974), pp. 225-249.
Deardorff, Alan. "The Optimum Growth Rate for Popu-
lation: Comment." International Economic Review
Vol. 17 (June 1976), pp. 510-516.
Diamond, Peter. "A Framework for Social Security
Analysis." Journal of Public Economics. Vol. 8
(1977), pp. 275-298.
Diamond, Peter and Mirrlees, J. "A Model of Social
Insurance With Variable Retirement." Journal of
Public Economics. Vol. 10 (1978), pp. 295-336.
Domar, Evsey. "The Burden of Debt and the National
Income." American Economic Review. Vol. 34
(December 1944), pp. 798-827.

Donaldson, David. "On the Optimal Mix of Social Insu-
rance Payments." in Old Age Income Assurance,
Part III: Public Programs. Joint Economic
Committee, 90th Congress, 1st Session. Washington,
D.C.: Government Printing Office, 1967.
Dreze, J.H. "Market Allocation Under Uncertainty."
European Economic Review, Vol. 2 (Winter 1970-71),
pp. 133-165.
Eisner, Robert. "Capital Shortage: Myth and Reality."
American Economic Review: Papers and Proccedings.
Vol. 67 (February 1977), pp. 110-115.
Feldstein, Martin. "Tax Incentives, Corporate Savings,
and Capital Accumulation in the United States."
Journal of Public Economic. Vol. 2 (April 1973),
pp. 159-171.
_____. "Social Security Induced Retirement, and
Aggregate Capital Accumulation." Journal of
Political Economy, Vol. 82 (September/October
1974), pp. 905-926.
_____. "Toward a Reform of Social Security."
Public Interest. Vol. 40 (Summer 1975), pp.75-95.
_____. "Social Security and Saving: The Extended
Life Cycle Theory." American Economic Review:
Papers and Proceedings, Vol. 66 (May 1976), pp.
77-86.
_____. "The Social Security Fund and National
Capital Accumulation." in Funding Pensions:
Issues and Implications for Financial Markets.
Federal Reserve Bank of Boston, Conference Series,
No. 16, October 1976.
_____. "Social Security and the Distribution of
Wealth." Journal of American Statistical Associ-
ation. Vol. 71 (December 1976), pp. 800-807.
_____. "Does the United States Save Too Little?"
American Economic Review: Papers and Proceedings.
Vol. 67 (February 1977), pp. 116-121.
_____. "National Saving in the United States."
in Capital for Productivity and Jobs. The
American Assembly. Englewood Cliffs, N.J.:
Prentice Hall, 1977.
_____. "Social Insurance" in Income Redistribu-
tion. Edited by C.D. Campbell. Washington, D.C.:
American Enterprise Institute, 1977.
_____. "Social Security and Private Savings:
International Evidence in an Extended Life-Cycle
Model." in The Economics of Public Services.
Edited by M. Feldstein and R. Inman. Internation-
al Economic Association Series, 1977.
_____. "Do Private Pensions Increase National
Savings?" Journal of Public Economics. Vol. 10
(1978), pp. 277-293.

174

_____. The Effect of Social Security on Saving.
National Bureau of Economic Research, Working
Paper, No. 334, April 1979.
_____. "Discussion." Social Security Bulletin,
Vol. 42 (May 1979), pp. 36-39.
_____. Government Deficits and Aggregate Demand.
National Bureau of Economic Research, Working
Paper No. 435, January 1980.
Feldstein, Martin and Pellechio, Anthony. Social
Security Wealth: The Impact of Alternative
Inflation Adjustments. National Bureau of
Economic Research, Working Paper No. 212,
November 1977.
_____. "Social Security and Household Wealth
Accumulation: New Microeconomic Evidence".
Review of Economics and Statistics. Vol. 61
(August 1979), pp. 361-368.
Feldstein, Martin and Summers, Lawrence. "Is the
Rate of Profit Falling?" Brookings Papers in
Economic Activity. Vol. 1 (1977), pp. 211-227.
Friedman, Benjamin. "Public Pension Funding and U.S.
Capital Formation: A Medium Run View." In
Funding Pensions: Issues and Implications for
Financial Markets, Federal Reserve Bank of
Boston, Conference Series No. 16, October 1976.
Furstenberg, G. M. Von. "The Effect of the Changing
Size and Composition of Government Purchases on
Potential Output." Review of Economics and
Statistics. Vol. LXII (February 1980), pp.74-80.
Furstenberg, G.M. Von, and Malkiel, Burton. "The
Government and Capital Formation: A Survey of
Recent Issues." Journal of Economic Literature,
Vol. 15 (September 1977), pp. 835-878.
Greene, Kenneth V. "Toward a Positive Theory of
Intergenerational Income Transfers." Public
Finance, Vol. 29 (1974), pp. 306-323.
Hemming, Richard. "The Effect of State and Private
Pensions on Retirement Behavior and Personal
Capital Accumulation." Review of Economic
Studies, Vol. 44 (1977), pp. 169-172.
_____. "State Pensions and Personal Savings."
Scottish Journal of Political Economy, Vol. 25
(June 1978), pp. 135-148.
Hirshleifer, J and Riley, J.G. "The Analytics of
Uncertainty and Information - An Expository
Survey." Journal of Economic Literature, Vol.
17 (December 1979), pp. 1375-1421.
Hogan, T.D. "The Implications of Population Statio-
narity for the Social Security System". Social
Science Quarterly, Vol. LV (June 1974), pp.
151-158.

Horlick, Max. "Administrative Costs for Social Security Programs in Selected Countries." Social Security Bulletin. Vol. 39 (June 1976), pp. 31 and 56.

Hu Sheng, C. "On the Dynamic Behavior of the Consumer and the Optimal Provision of Social Security", Review of Economics and Statistics. Vol. XVL(3) (October 1978), pp. 437-446.

Kaplan, Robert. "A Comparison of Rates of Return to Social Security Retirees under Wage and Price Indexing." in Financing Social Security, edited by C.D. Campbell. Washington, D.C.: American Enterprise Institute, 1979.

Katona, George. Private Pensions and Individual Saving. Survey Research Center, University of Michigan, 1965.

Kihlstrom, R. and Pauly, M. "The Role of Insurance in the Allocation of Risk." American Economic Review (Papers and Proceedings). Vol. 61 (May 1971), pp. 371-379.

Kirkpatrick, E.K. "The Revaluation of Earnings Records in the Social Security Systems in Six Countries." International Social Security Review. Vol. 31 (1978), pp. 293+.

Kochin, L. "Are Future Taxes Anticipated by Consumers?" Journal of Money, Credit, and Banking. Vol. 6 (August 1974), pp. 385-394.

Kopits, George and Gotur, Padma. "The Influence of Social Security on Household Savings: A Cross-Country Investigation." International Monetary Fund Staff Papers, Vol. 27 (March 1980).

Kotlikoff, L.J. "Social Security and Equilibrium Capital Intensity." Quarterly Journal of Economics. Vol. 93 (May 1979), pp. 233-253.

_____. "Testing the Theory of Social Security and Life Cycle Accumulation." American Economic Review. Vol. 69 (June 1979), pp. 396-410.

Kurz, M. and Avrin, M. "Current Issues of the U.S. Pension System." Mimeograph. Prepared for the President's Commission on Pension Policy, June 1979.

Layard, Richard. "On Measuring the Redistribution of Lifetime Income." in The Economics of Public Services. Edited by M. Feldstein and R. Inman. International Economic Association, Series, 1977.

Lazaer, E.P. "Why is There Mandatory Retirement?" Journal of Political Economy, Vol. 87 (December 1979), pp. 1261-1284.

Lerner, Abba. "The Burden of the National Debt." in Income, Employment and Public Policy: Essays in Honor of Alvin H. Hansen, edited by L. A. Metzler. New York: Norton Publishing Co., 1948.

176

_____ . "Consumption-Loan Interest and Money."
Journal of Political Economy. Vol. 67 (October
1959), pp. 512-525.
Levy, M.D. "The Case for Extending Social Security
Coverage to Government Employees." Journal of
Risk and Insurance. Vol. XLVII (March 1980),
pp. 78-90.
Logue, Dennis. "How Social Security May Undermine
the Private Industrial Pension System." in
Financing Social Security, edited by C.D. Camp-
bell. Washington, D.C.: American Enterprise
Institute, 1979.
MacRae, D.C. and MacRae, E.C. "Labor Supply and the
Payroll Tax." American Economic Review. Vol.
66 (June 1976), pp. 408-409.
Marshall, John. "Insurance as a Market in Contingent
Claims." Bell Journal of Economics and Manage-
ment Science, Vol. 5 (Autumn 1974), pp. 670-682.
_____ . "Insurance Theory: Reserves vs. Mutuality."
Western Economic Journal. Vol. 12 (December 1974)
pp. 476-492.
Meckling, W.H. "An Exact Consumption-Loan Model of
Interest: A Comment." Journal of Political
Economy. Vol. 68 (February 1960), pp. 72-76.
Mirer, T.W. "The Wealth-Age Relations Among the
Aged." American Economic Review. Vol. 69 (June
1979), pp. 435-443.
Morishima, M. and Saito, M. "A Dynamic Analysis of
the American Economy, 1902-1952." in The Work-
ings of Econometric Models, edited by M. Morishi-
ma, et al. London: Cambridge University Press,
1972.
Munnell, Alicia. The Effect of Social Security on
Personal Savings. Cambridge: Ballinger Publish-
ing Co., 1974.
_____ . "The Impact of Social Security on Personal
Savings." National Tax Journal. Vol. 27 (Decem-
ber 1974), pp. 553-567.
_____ . "Private Pensions and Saving: New
Evidence." Journal of Political Economy. Vol.
85 (October 1976), pp. 1013-1032.
_____ . The Future of Social Security. Washington,
D.C.: Brookings Institution, 1977.
_____ . "The Future of the U.S. Pension System."
in Financing Social Security, edited by C.D.
Campbell. Washington, D.C.: American Enterprise
Institute, 1979, pp. 237-264.
Munnell, Alicia and Connolly, Ann. "Funding Govern-
ment Pensions: State-Local, Civil Service and
Military." in Funding Pensions: Issues and
Implications for Financial Markets. Federal
Reserve Bank of Boston, Conference Series No. 16,
October 1976.

177

Musgrave, Richard. The Theory of Public Finance. New York: McGraw Hill Book Co., 1959.
_____. "The Role of Social Insurance in an Overall Program for Social Welfare." in The American System of Social Insurance: Its Philosophy, Impact, and Future Development. New York: McGraw Hill, 1968.
_____. "Tax Policy and Capital Formation." National Tax Journal. Vol. 32 (September 1979), pp. 351-357.
Myers, Robert. "Administrative Expenses in the Social Security Program." Social Security Bulletin, Vol. 31 (September 1969), pp. 20-27.
Oldfield, G.S. "Financial Aspects of the Private Pension System." Journal of Money, Credit, and Banking. Vol. 9 (February 1977), pp. 48-54.
Peacock, Alan T. "Social Security and Inflation: A Study of the Economic Effects of an Adjustable Pensions Scheme." Review of Economic Studies. Vol. 20 (1952-1953), pp. 169-173.
Pechman, J., Aaron, H., Taussig, M. Social Security: Perspectives for Reform, Brookings Studies in Social Economics. Washington, D.C.: Brookings Institutiton, 1968.
Pellechio, Anthony. The Effects of Social Security on Retirement. National Bureau of Economic Research, Working Paper 260, July 1978.
_____. The Social Security Earnings Test, Labor Supply Distortions, and Foregone Payroll Tax Revenues, National Bureau of Economic Research, Working Paper No. 272, August 1978.
_____. "Social Security Financing and Retirement Behavior." American Economic Review: Papers and Proceedings. Vol. 69 (May 1979), pp. 284-287.
Pesando, J.E. and Rea, S.A. Public and Private Pensions in Canada: An Economic Analysis. Ontario Economic Council Research Studies, No. 9. Toronto and Buffalo: University of Toronto Press, 1977.
Peterson, R.M. "Misconceptions and Missing Perspectives of our Social Security System." Transactions of the Society of Actuaries, Vol. 11 (November 1959), pp. 812-851.
Phelps, Edmund and Shell, Karl. "Public Debt,Taxation, and Capital Intensiveness." Journal of Economic Theory. Vol. 1 (October 1969), pp. 330-346.
Pitts, A.M. "Social Security and Aging Population." in The Economic Consequences of Slowing Population Growth, edited by T.J. Espenshade and W.J. Serow. New York: Academic Press, 1978.
Pogue, T.F. and Sgontz, L.G. "Social Security and Investment in Human Capital." National Tax Journal. Vol. 30 (June 1977), pp. 157-169.

Praag, Bernard, and Poeth, Guy. "The Introduction of an Old-Age Pension in a Growing Economy". Journal of Public Economics. Vol. 4 (1975), pp. 87-100.

Prest, A.R. "Comments." National Tax Journal. Vol. 22 (December 1969), pp. 554-556.

Rejda, George and Schmidt, J.R. "The Impact of the Social Security Program on Private Pension Contributions." Journal of Risk and Insurance. Vol. 46 (December 1979), pp. 636-651.

Rejda, George and Shepler, R. "The Impact of Zero Population Growth on the OASDHI Program". Journal of Risk and Insurance, Vol. 40 (September 1973), pp. 313-325.

Richardson, Henry J. Economic and Financial Aspects of Social Security. Toronto: University of Toronto Press, 1960.

Rohrlich, George. "The Place of Social Insurance in the Pursuit of the General Welfare." Journal of Risk and Insurance. Vol. 36 (September 1969), pp. 333-353.

Samuelson, Paul A. "An Exact Consumption-Loan Model of Interest With or Without the Social Contrivance of Money." Journal of Political Economy. Vol. 66 (December 1958), pp. 467-482.

_____. "Infinity, Unanimity, and Singularity: A Reply." Journal of Political Economy. Vol. 68 (February 1960), pp. 76-84.

_____. "The Optimum Growth Rate for Population." International Economic Review. Vol. 16 (October 1975), pp. 531-537.

_____. "Optimum Social Security in a Life-Cycle Growth Model." International Economic Review. Vol. 16 (October 1975), pp. 539-544.

_____. "The Optimum Growth Rate for Population: Agreement and Evaluations." International Economic Review. Vol. 17 (June 1976), pp. 516-525.

Schulz, J.H. "Public Policy and the Future Roles of Public and Private Pensions." in Income Support for the Aged, edited by G.S. Tolley and R.V. Burkhauser. Cambridge, Mass.: Ballinger Publishing Co., 1977.

Schulz, J.H. and Carrin, G. "The Role of Savings and Pension Systems in Maintaining Living Standards in Retirement." Journal of Human Resources. Vol. 7 (Summer 1972), pp. 343-365.

Shenshinski, Eytan. "A Model of Social Security and Retirement Decisions." Journal of Public Economics. Vol. 10 (1978), pp. 337-360.

Shoup, Carl. "Debt Financing and Future Generations." Economic Journal. Vol. 72 (1962), pp. 887-898.

Sobol, M.G. "Factors Influencing Private Capital Accumulation on the Eve of Retirement". Review of Economics and Statistics. Vol. LXI (November 1979), pp. 585-593.

Spence, Michael. "Product Differentiation and Performance in Insurance Markets." Journal of Public Economics. Vol. 10 (1978), pp. 427-447.

Spengler, Joseph. "Population Aging and Security of The Aged." Atlantic Economic Journal. Vol. 6 (March 1978), pp. 1-7.

_____. Facing Zero Population Growth. Durham, N. C.: Duke University Press, 1978.

Stahlberg, Ann-Charlotte. "Effects of the Swedish Supplementary Pension System on Personal and Aggregate Household Saving." Scandinavian Journal of Economics. Vol. 82 (1980), pp. 25-44.

Steiner, P.O. "Public Expenditure Budgeting" in The Economics of Public Finance, edited by A. Blinder, R. Solow, et al. Washington, D.C.: The Brookings Institution, 1974.

Tanner, J.E. "An Empirical Test of the Extent of Tax Discounting: A Comment." Journal of Money,Credit,, and Banking. Vol. 11 (May 1979), pp. 214-218.

_____. "Fiscal Policy and Consumer Behavior." Review of Economics and Statistics. Vol. LXJ (May 1979), pp. 317-321.

Thompson, Earl. "Debt Instruments in Macroeconomic and Capital Theory." American Economic Review. Vol. 57 (December 1967), pp. 1196-1210.

Thompson, Lawrence and Water, Paul, Van de. "The Short Run Behavior of the Social Security Trust Funds." Public Finance Quarterly. Vol. 5 (July 1977), pp. 351-372.

U.S. Department of Health, Education and Welfare. Social Security Administration. Office of Research and Statistics. Internal Rates of Return to Retired, Worker Only Beneficiaries Under Social Security, 1967-1970, by A. Freiden, D.R. Leimer, and R. Hoffman. Studies in Income Distribution No. 5. Washington, D.C.: Government Printing Office, October 1976.

_____. Social Security Administration.Office of Research and Statistics. An Econometric Model of OASDI, by John Hambor. Studies in Income Distribution No. 10. Washington, D.C.: Government Printing Office, November 1978.

_____. Social Security Administration. Office of Research and Statistics. A Framework for Analyzing the Equity of the Social Security Benefit Structure, by D.R. Leimer, R. Hoffman, and A. Freiden. Studies in Income Distribution No. 6. Washington D.C.: Government Printing Office, January 1978.

_____. Social Security Administration. Office of

Research and Statistics. <u>Macroeconomic Effects</u>
<u>of Social Insurance on Aggregate Demand</u>, by
Wayne Vroman. Staff Paper No. 2. Washington
D.C.: Government Printing Office, July 1969.
_____. Social Security Administration. Office of
Research and Statistics. <u>Annual Statistical</u>
<u>Supplement of the Social Security Bulletin</u>, 1975,
1976.
_____. Social Security Administration. Office of
Research and Statistics. <u>Social Security Bulle-</u>
<u>tin</u>, monthly.
Weldon, J.C. "On the Theory of Intergenerational
    Transfers." <u>Canadian Journal of Economics</u>. Vol.
    9 (November 1976), pp. 559-579.
Winklevoss, H.E., McGill, D. <u>Public Pension Plans</u>:
    <u>Standards of Design, Funding, and Reporting</u>.
    Homewood, Illinois: Dow Jones-Irwin, 1979.
Young, Richard and Rimlinger, Gaston. "Mathematical
    Approaches to the Macroeconomics and Planning of
    Old-Age Pension Systems." in <u>Old-Age Income</u>
    <u>Assurance</u>, Part III: Public Programs, Joint
    Economic Committee, 90th Congress, 1st Session.
    Washington, D.C.: Government Printing Office,
    1967.

Index

182

about the length of
  retirement life, 20
decision-making under, 8
market, 7
resource allocation
  under, 7
risk and, 7
technological, 7
See also Risk

Von Newmann-Mergenstern
  function, 10